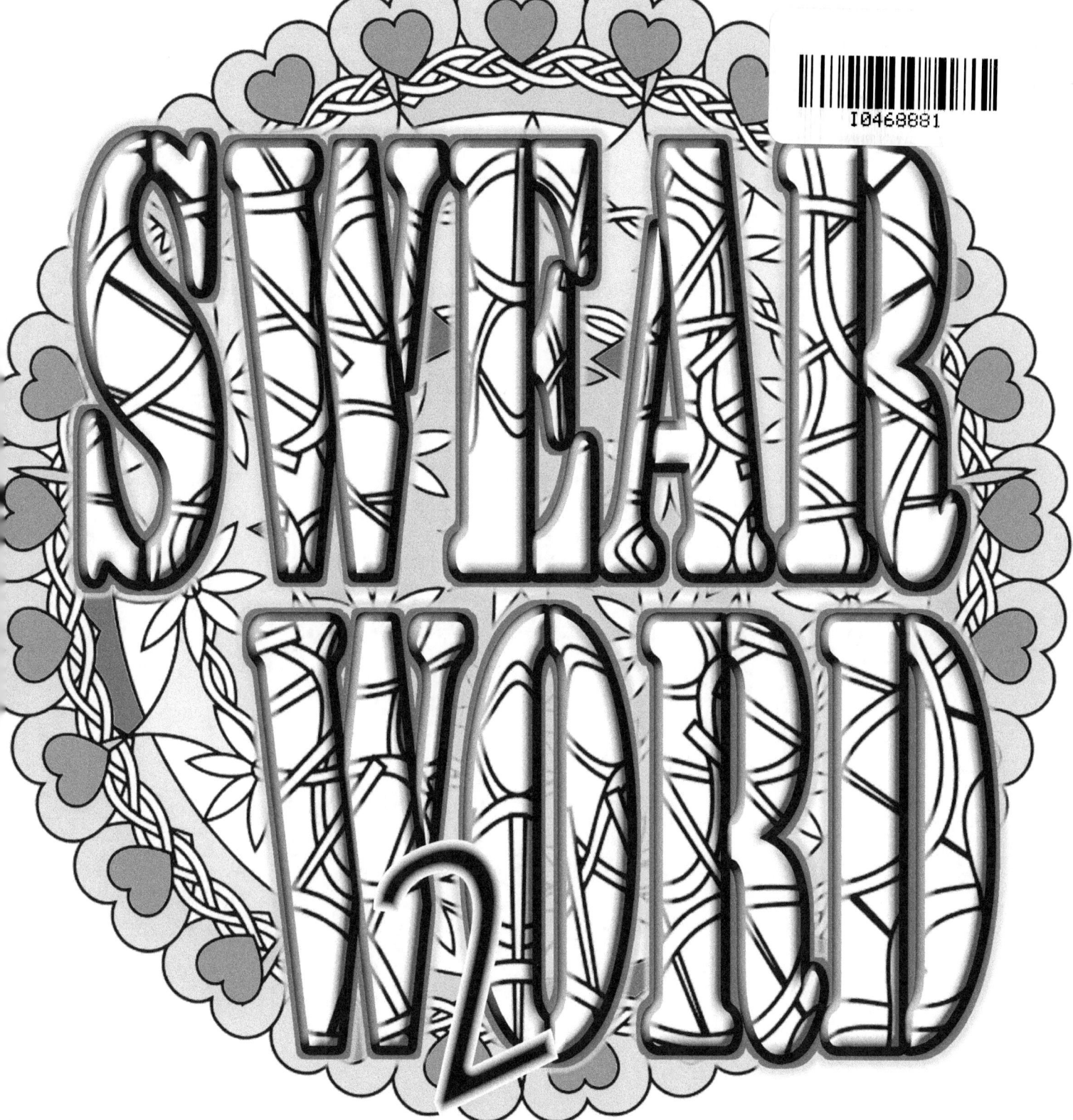

SWEAR WORD 2

ADULT COLORING BOOK

RELAX WITH CURSE WORDS

Life is full of things that stress us out. Between work, children, bills, and chores at home, our minds are inundated with stuff vying for our attention. Coloring is a great way to relax and allow stress to melt away.

Have a problem you are trying to figure out? Just open up this book, take your colored pencils, and begin filling in the blank spaces. Don't focus on anything, but coloring what is within this book. By doing this, you will clear you mind, and just might come up with the solution you've been searching for.

With 31+ swear words and designs to color,, this book has something for eery skill level. So just take a moment, relax, and color.

You can tear this page out and use it to put between the images so as to avoid bleed through.

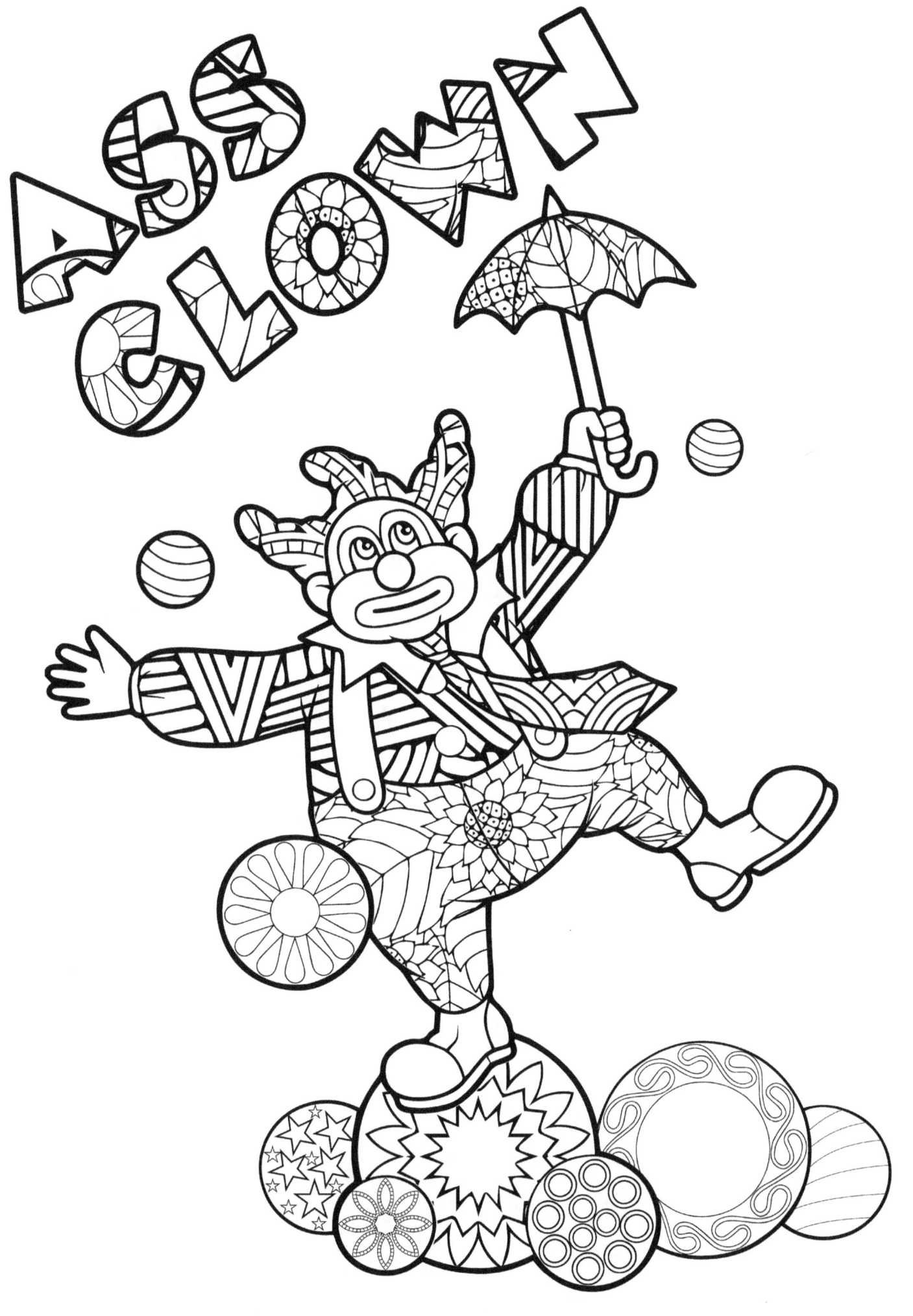

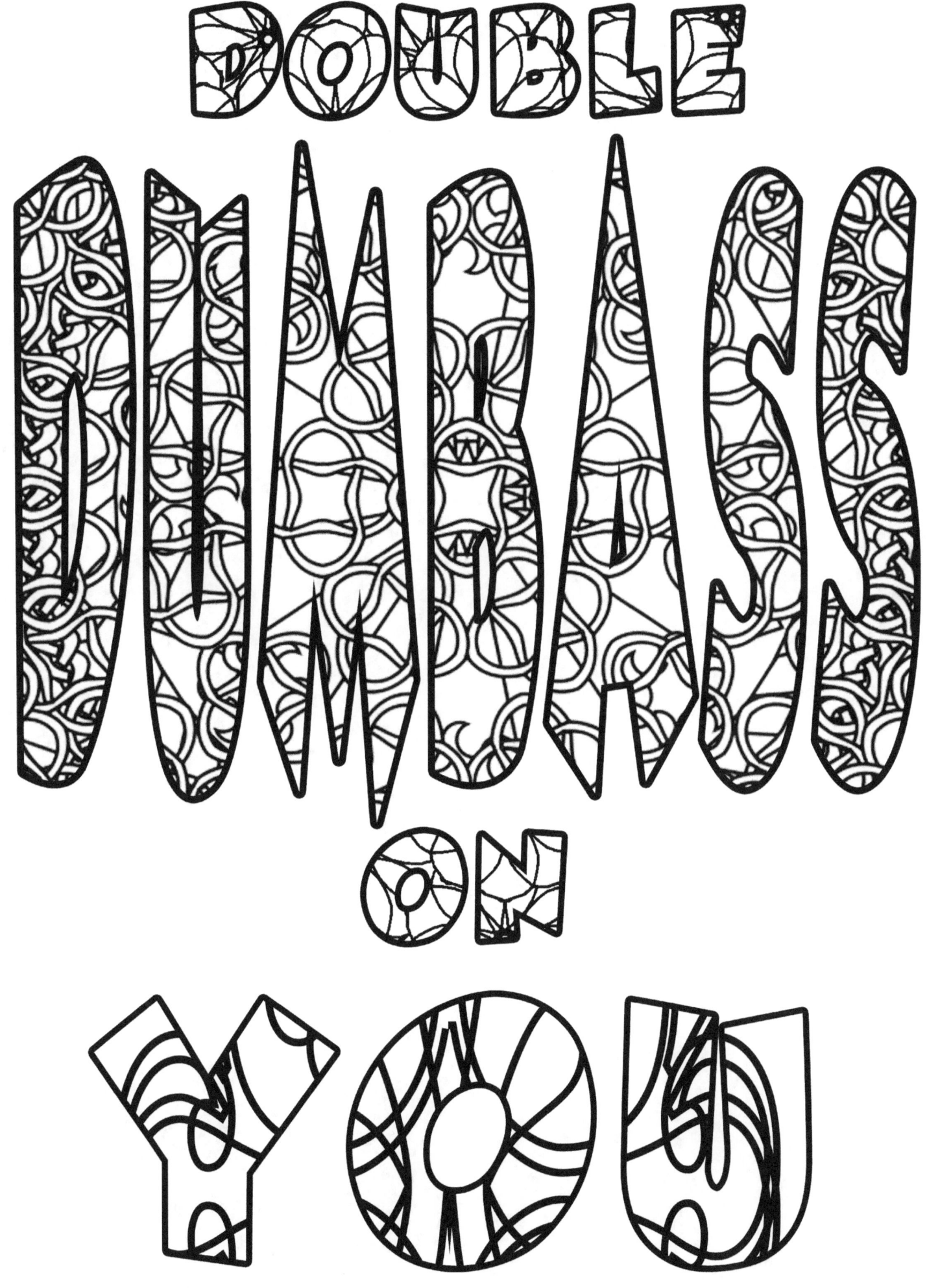

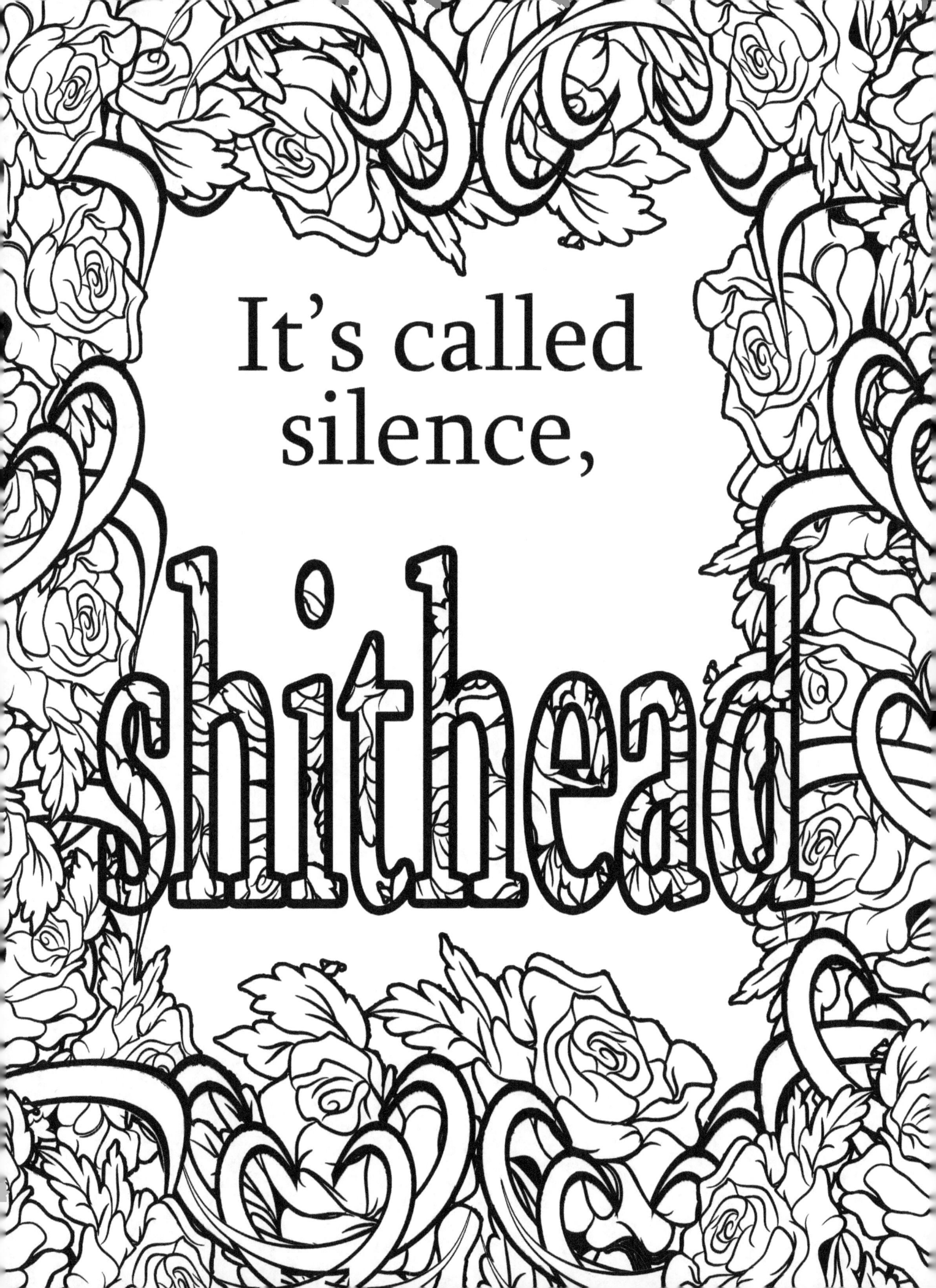

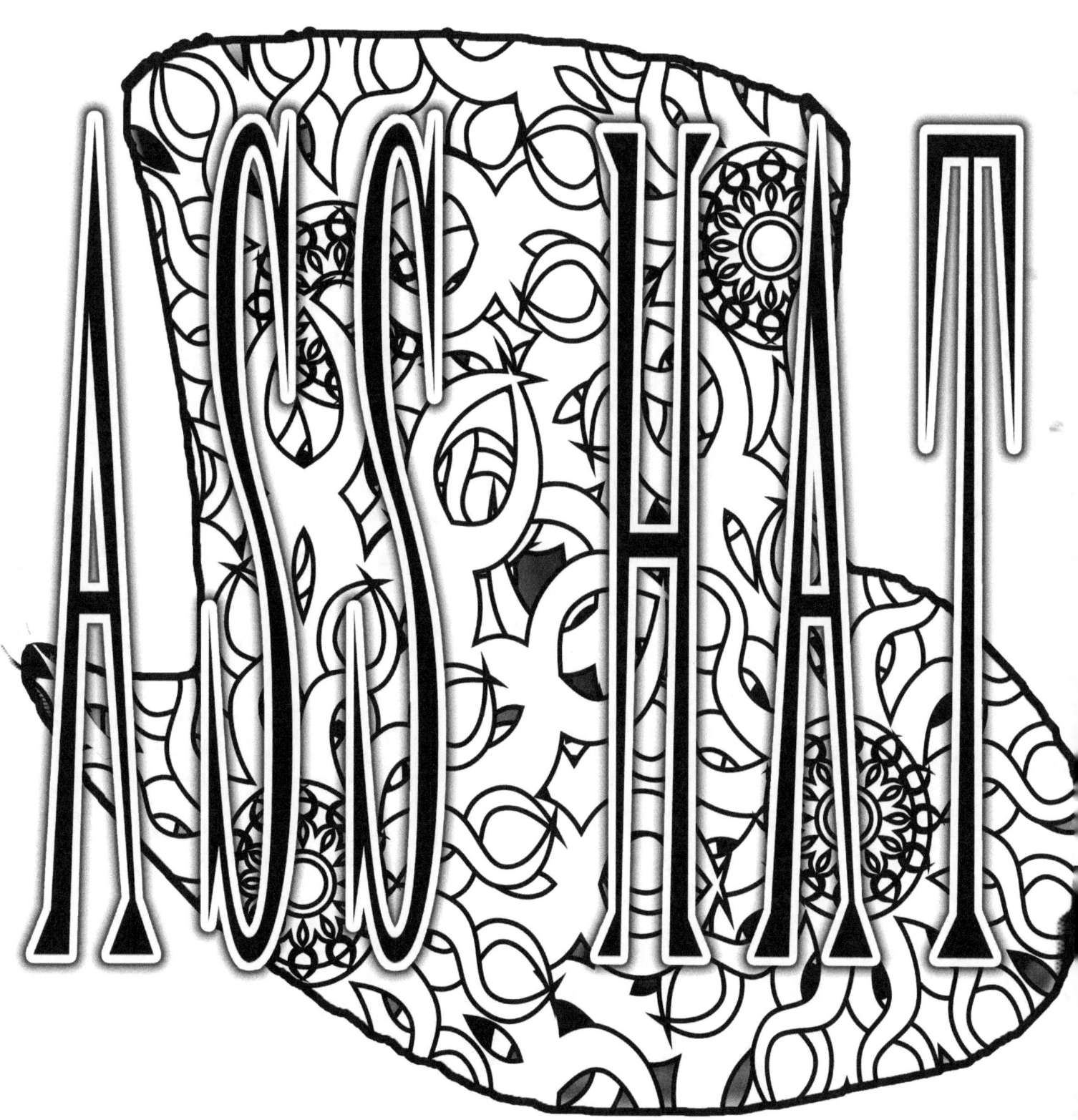

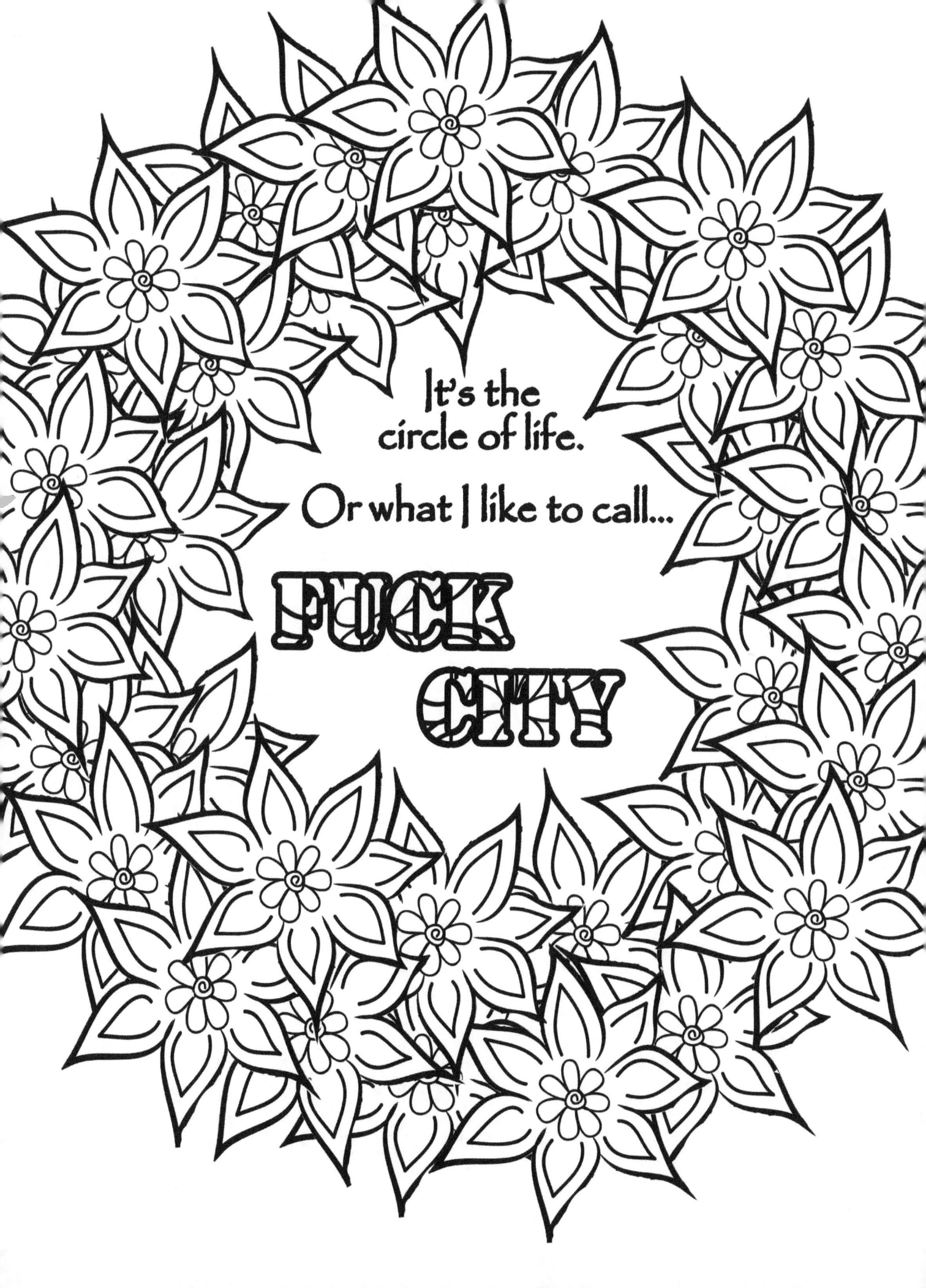

Can I offer you a
cup of I don't give a

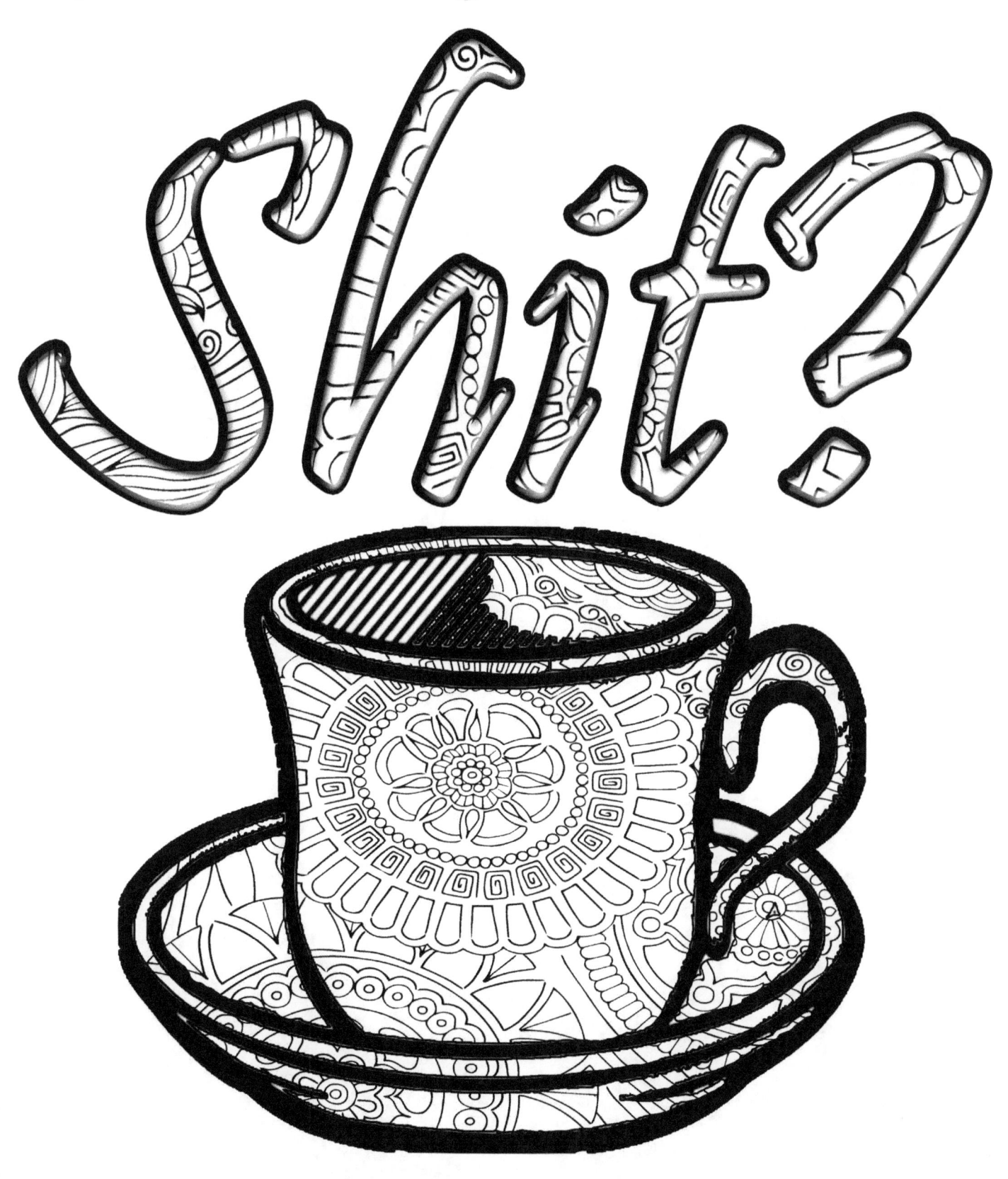

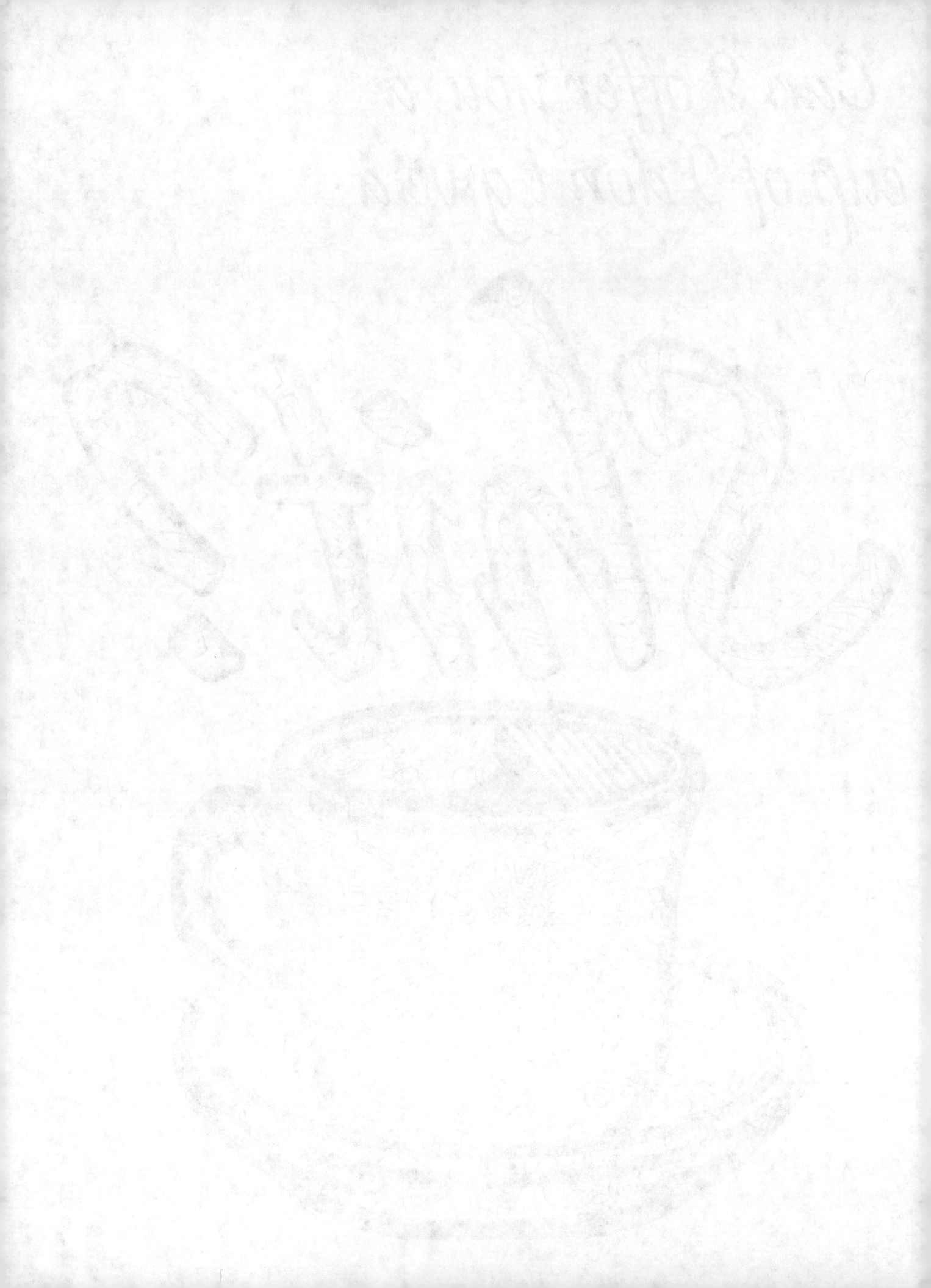

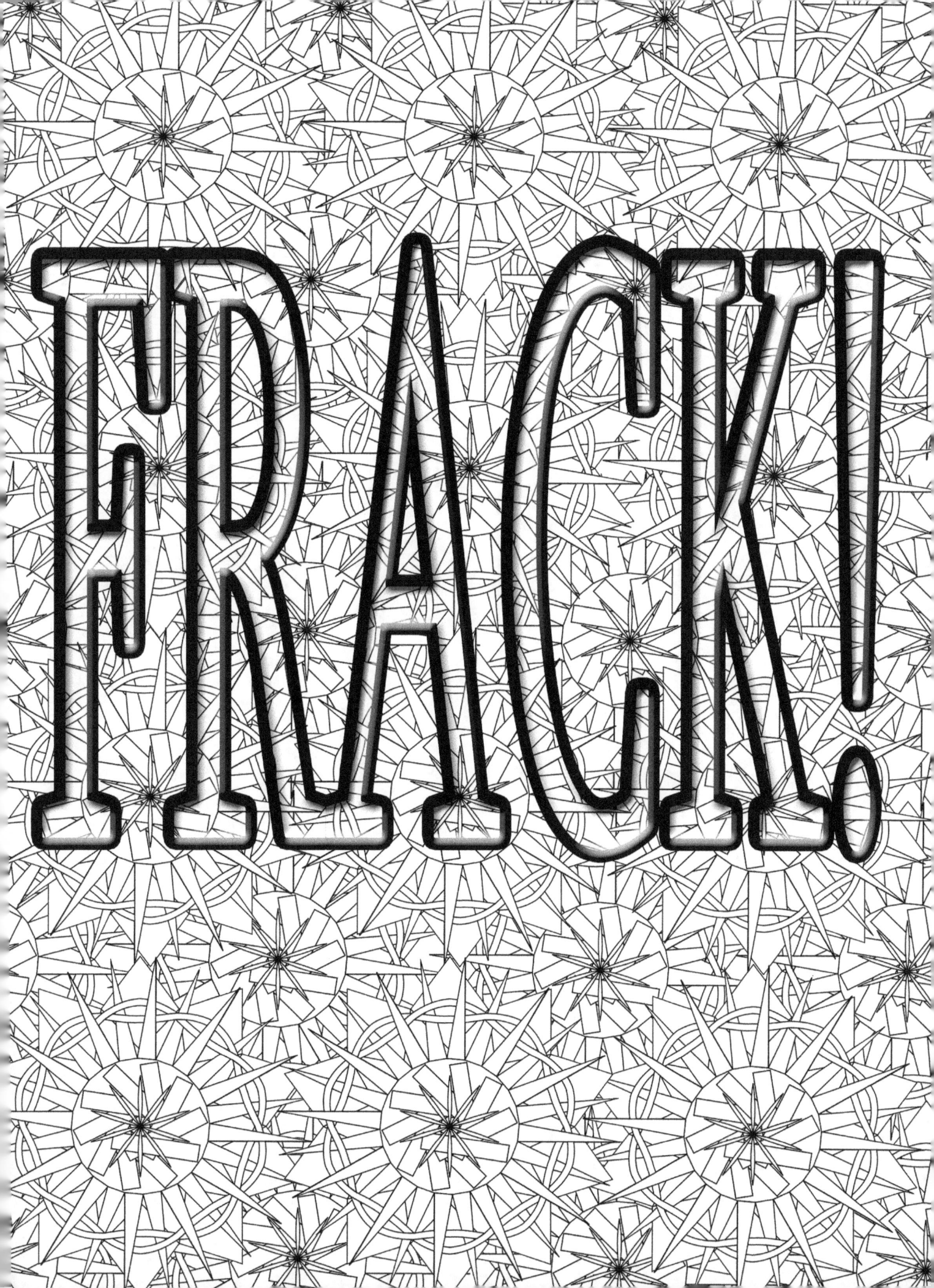

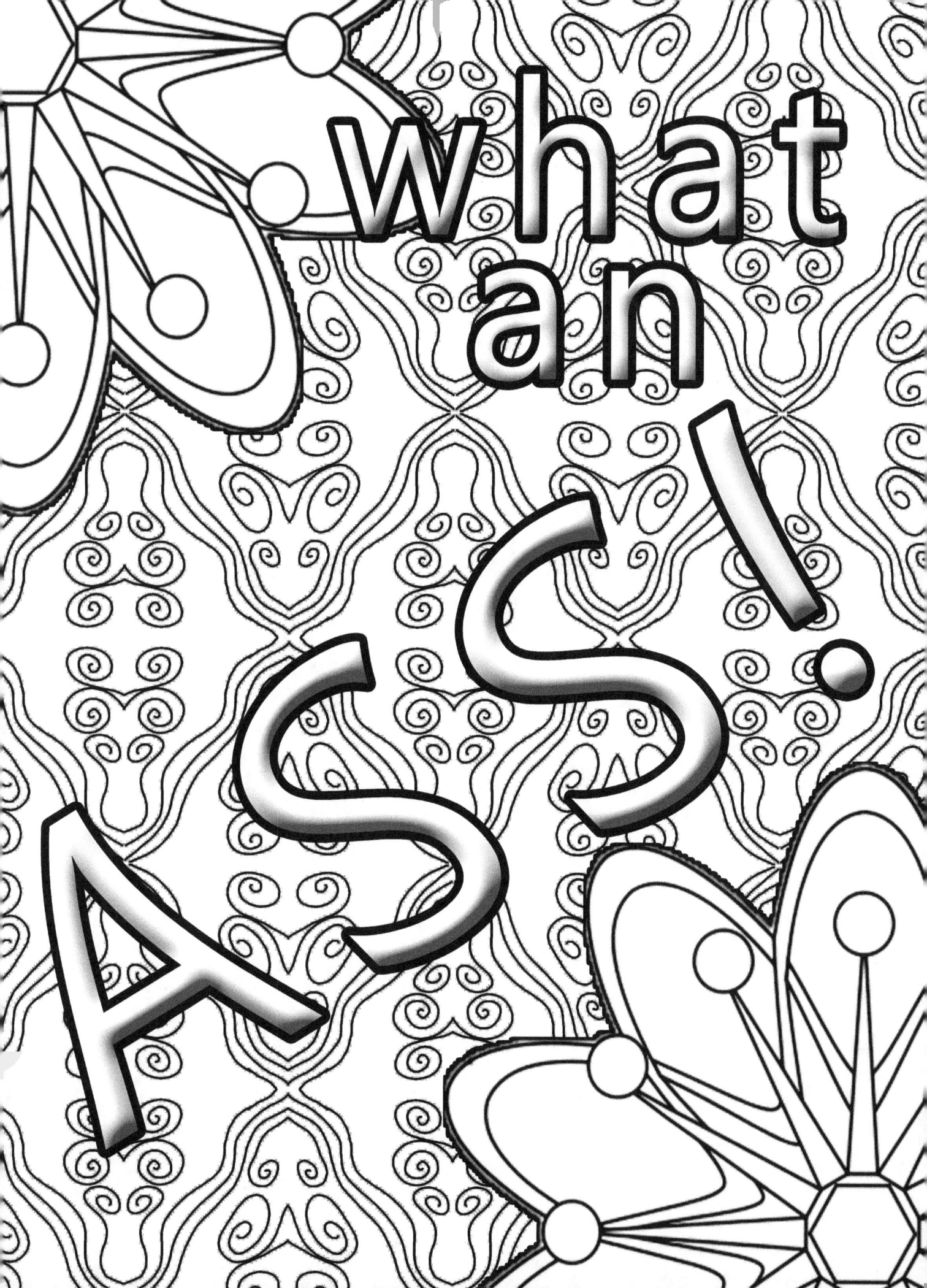

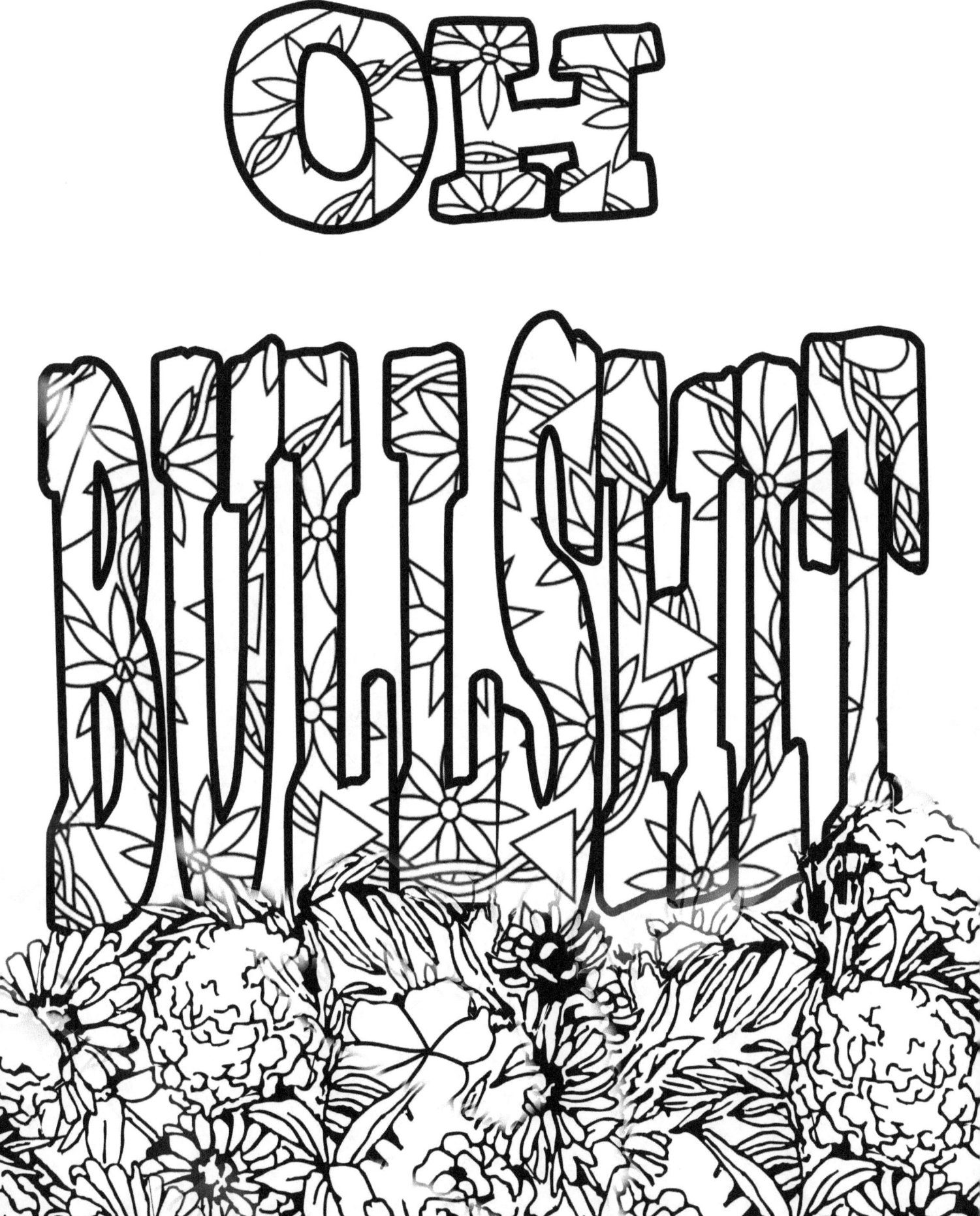

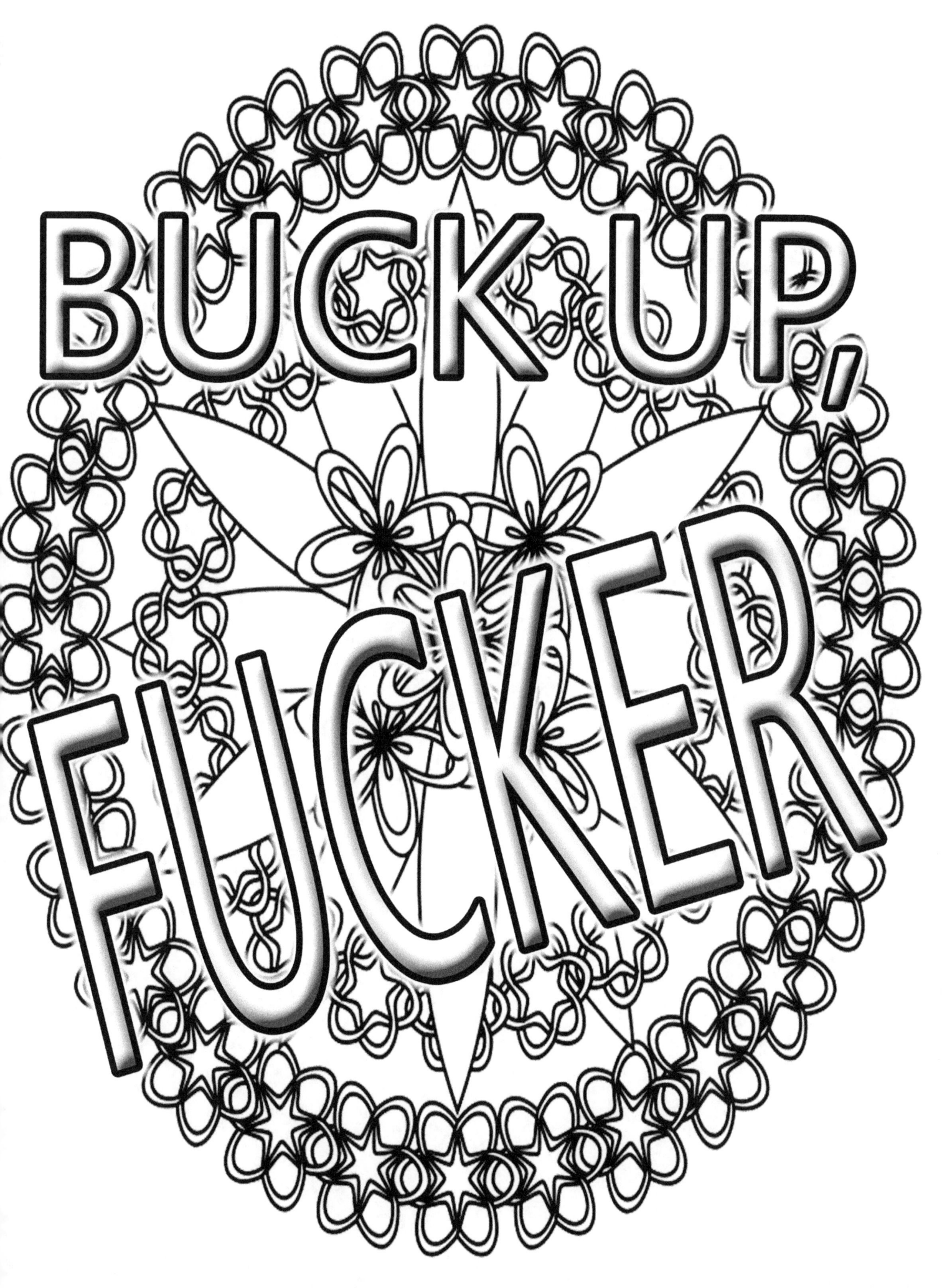

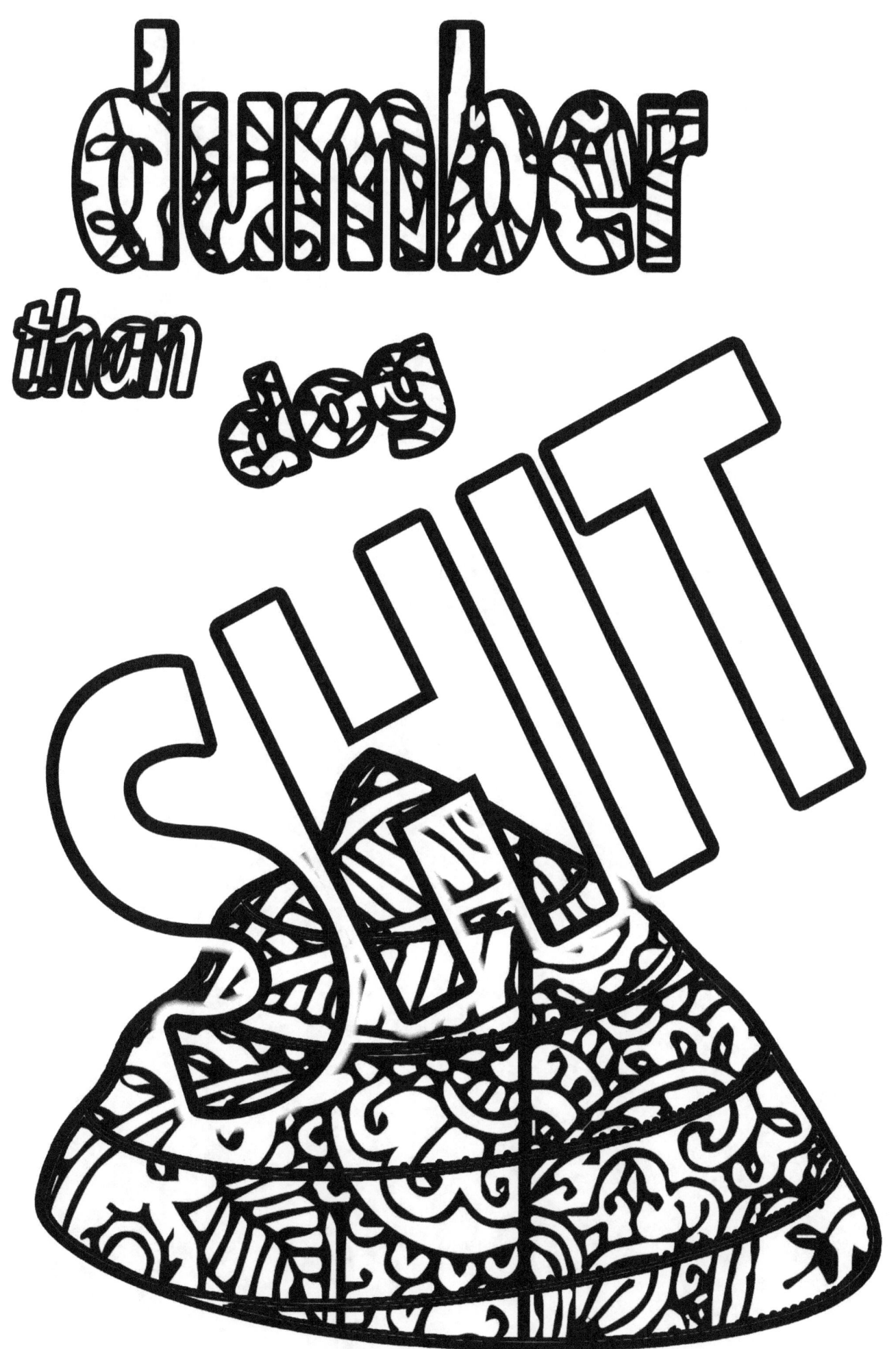

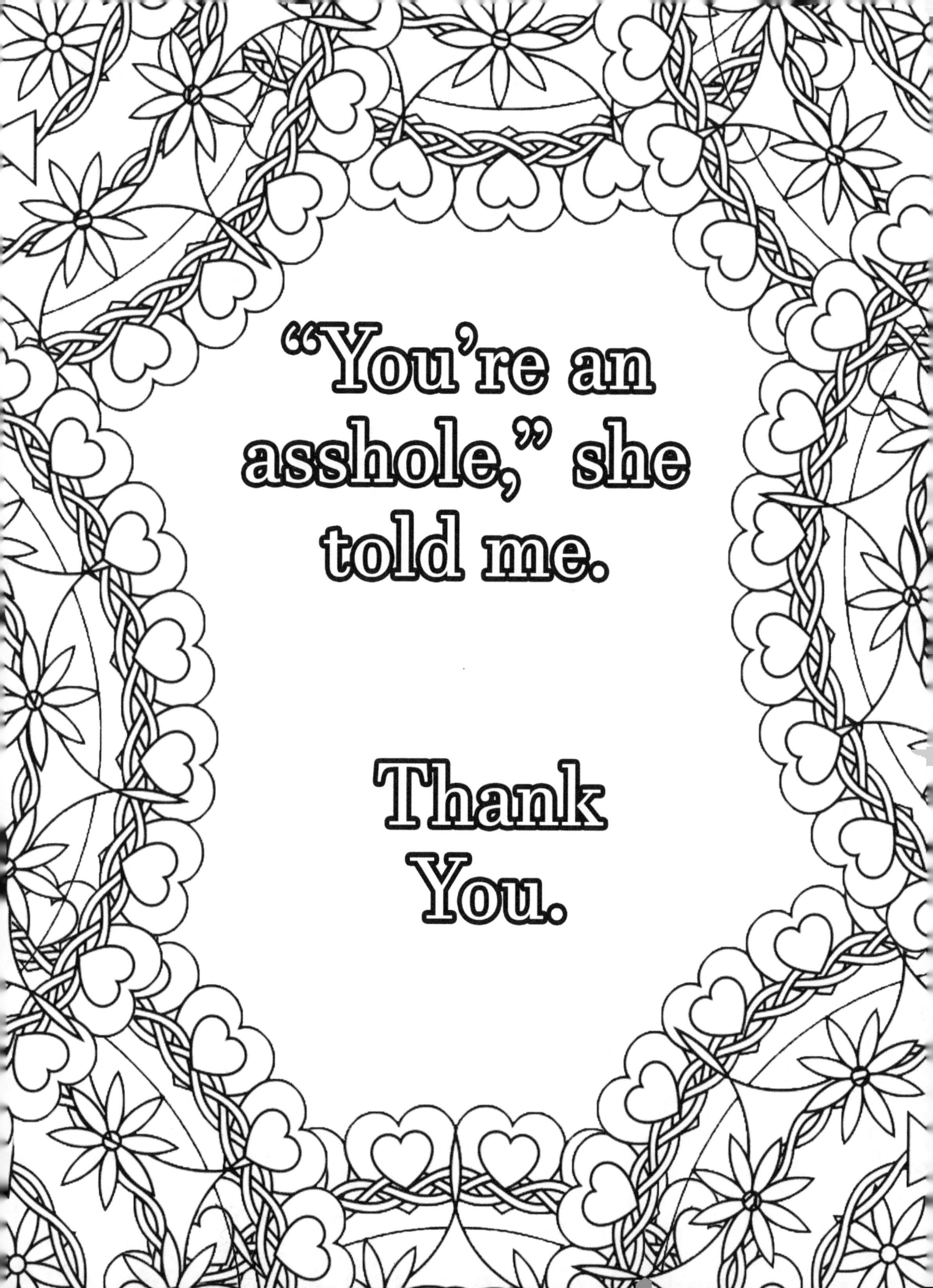

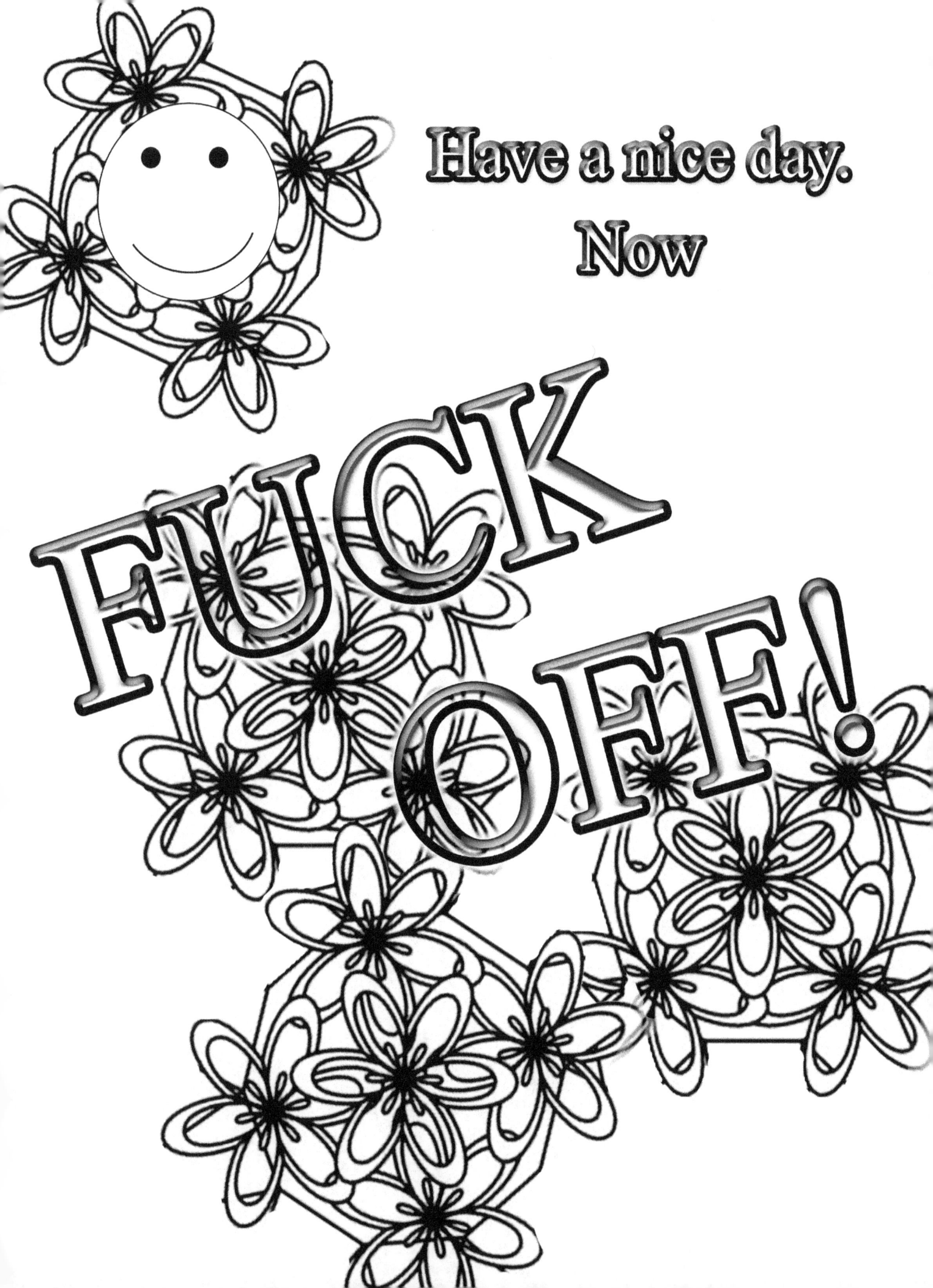

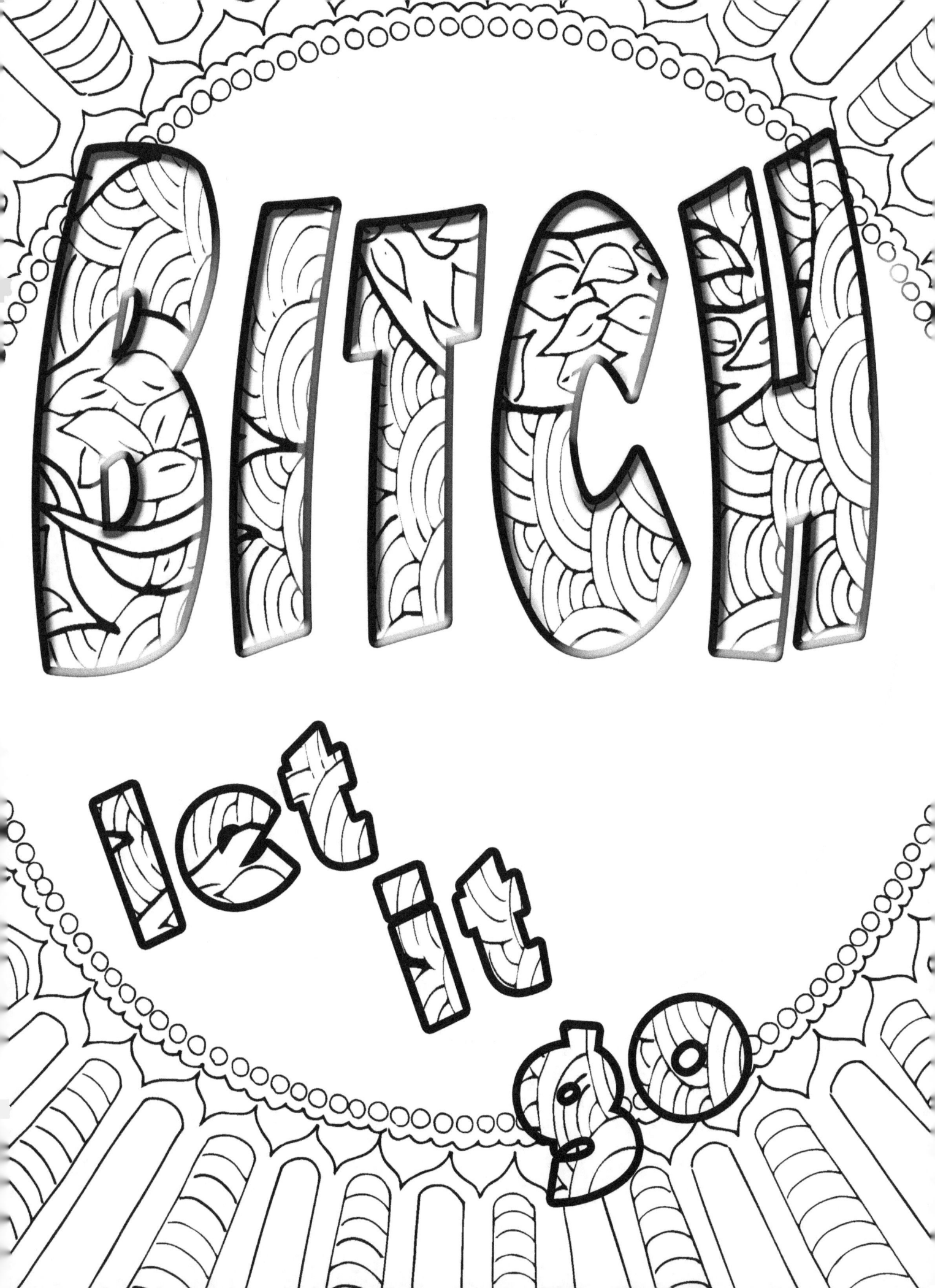

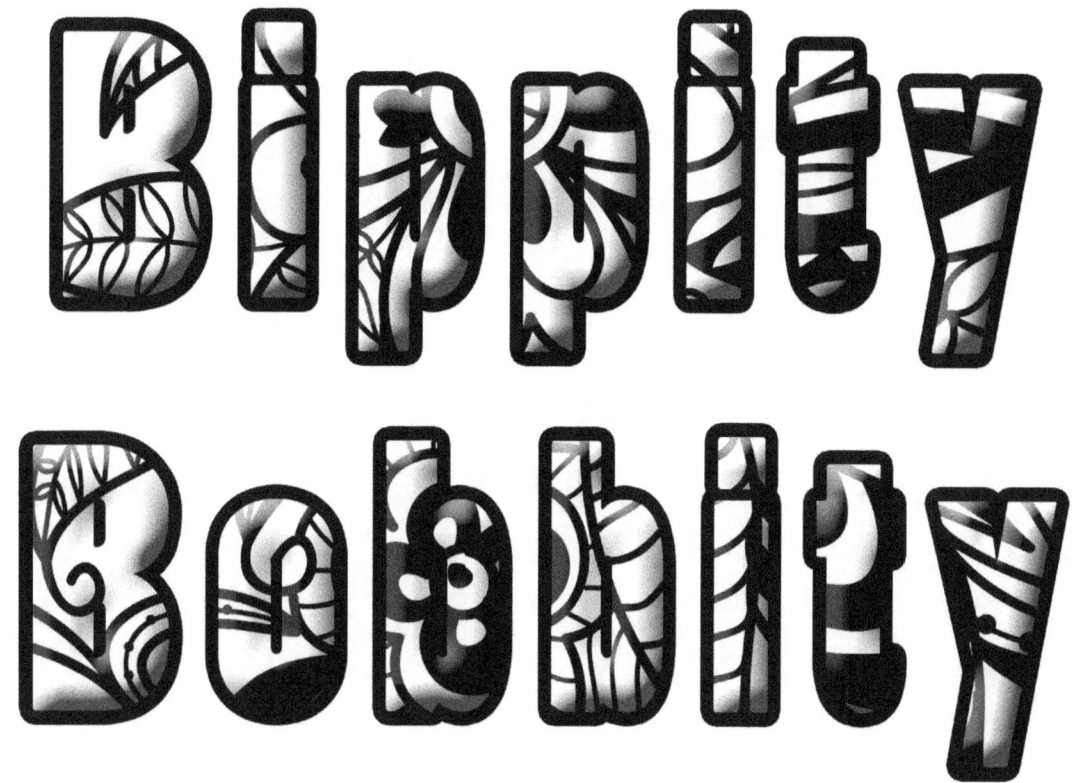

Bippity
Bobbity
DAMN

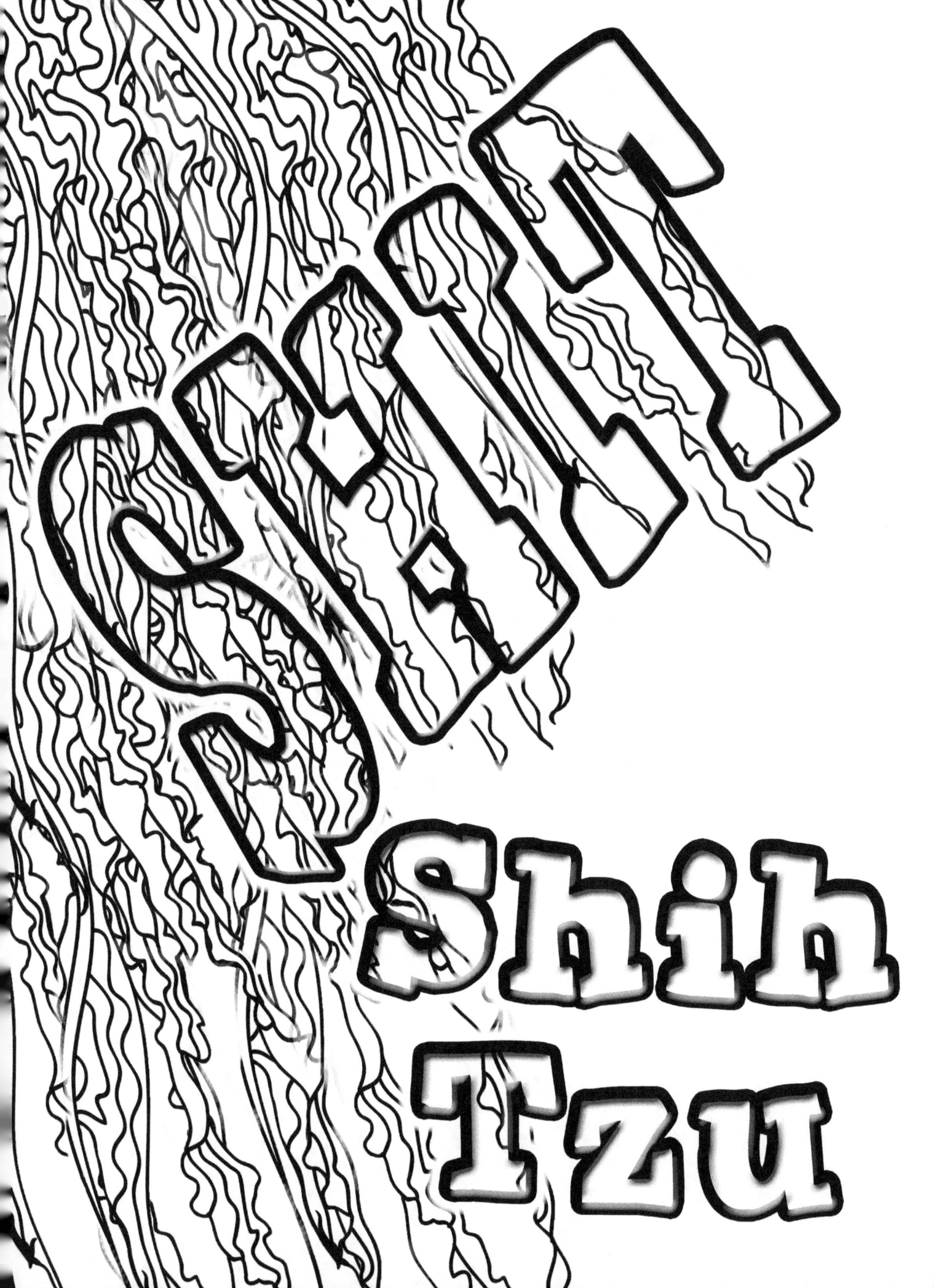

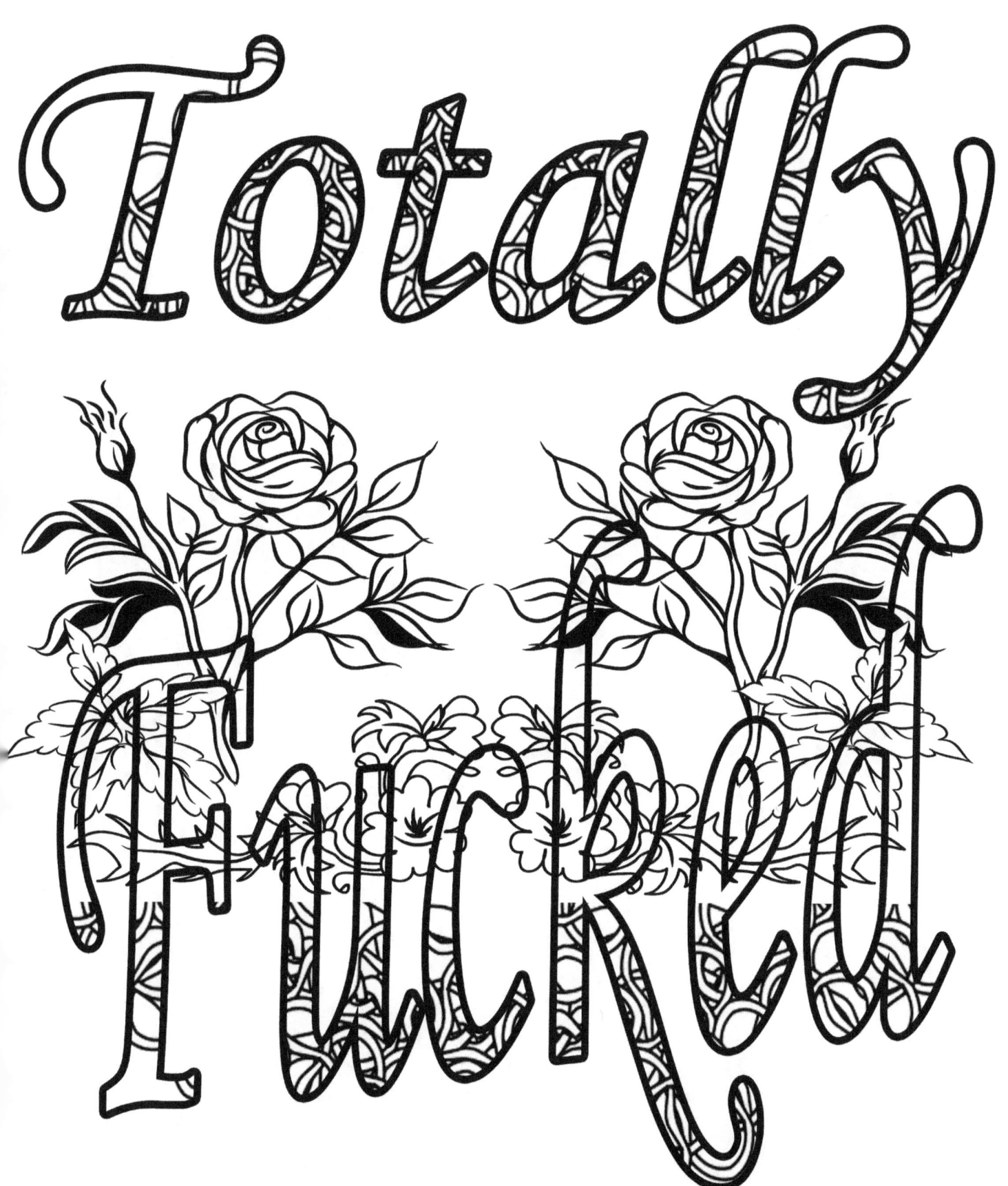

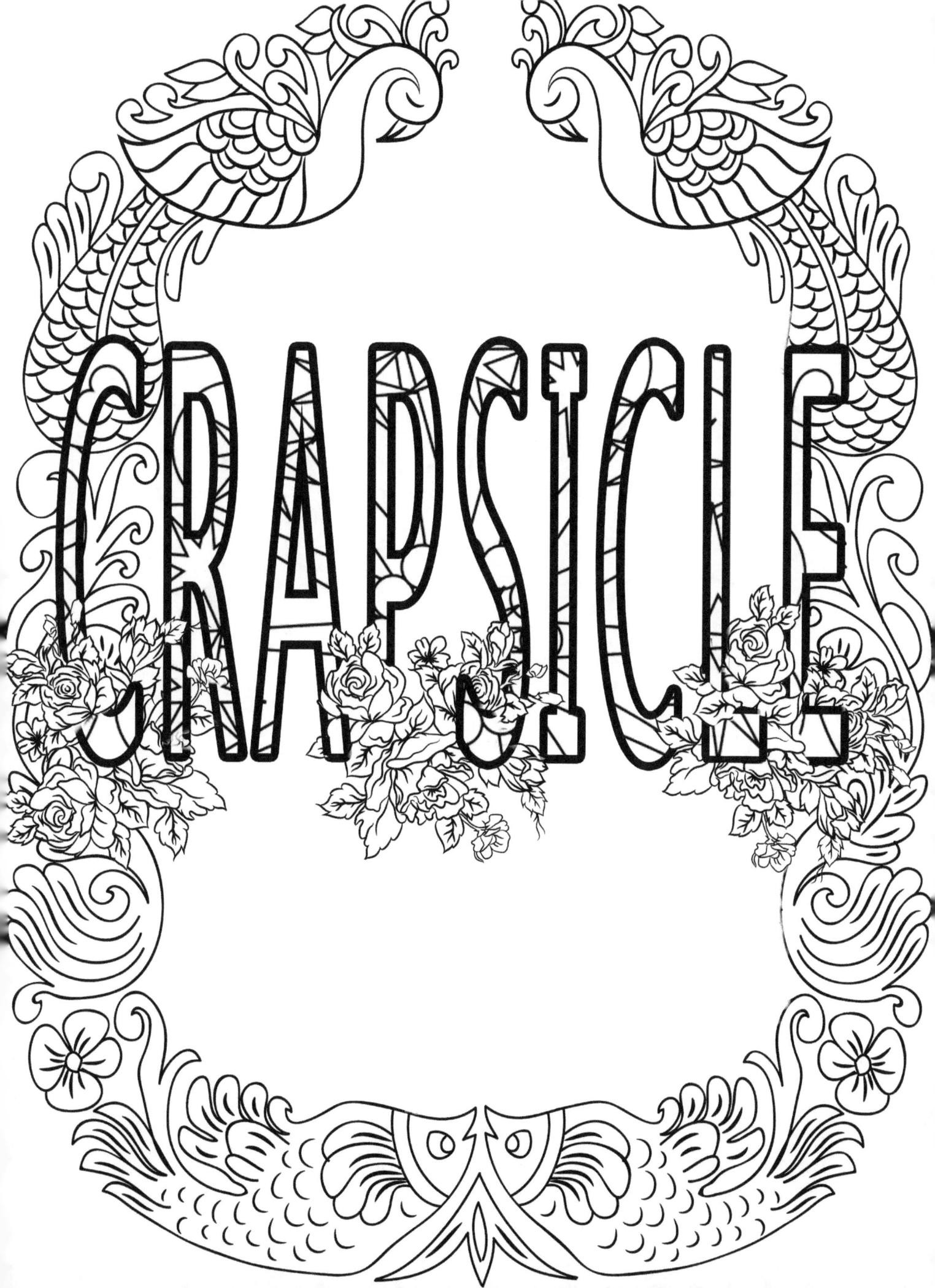

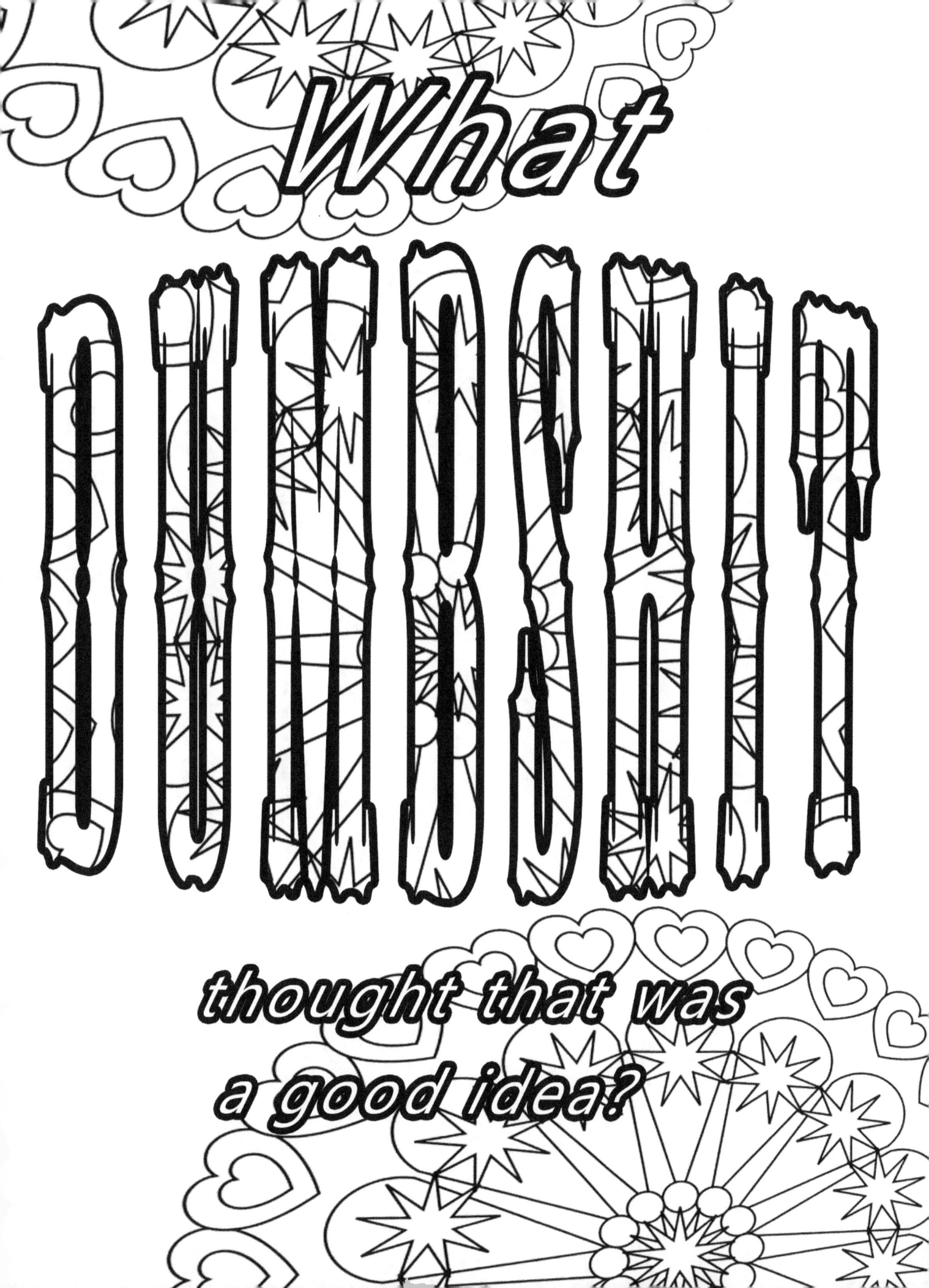

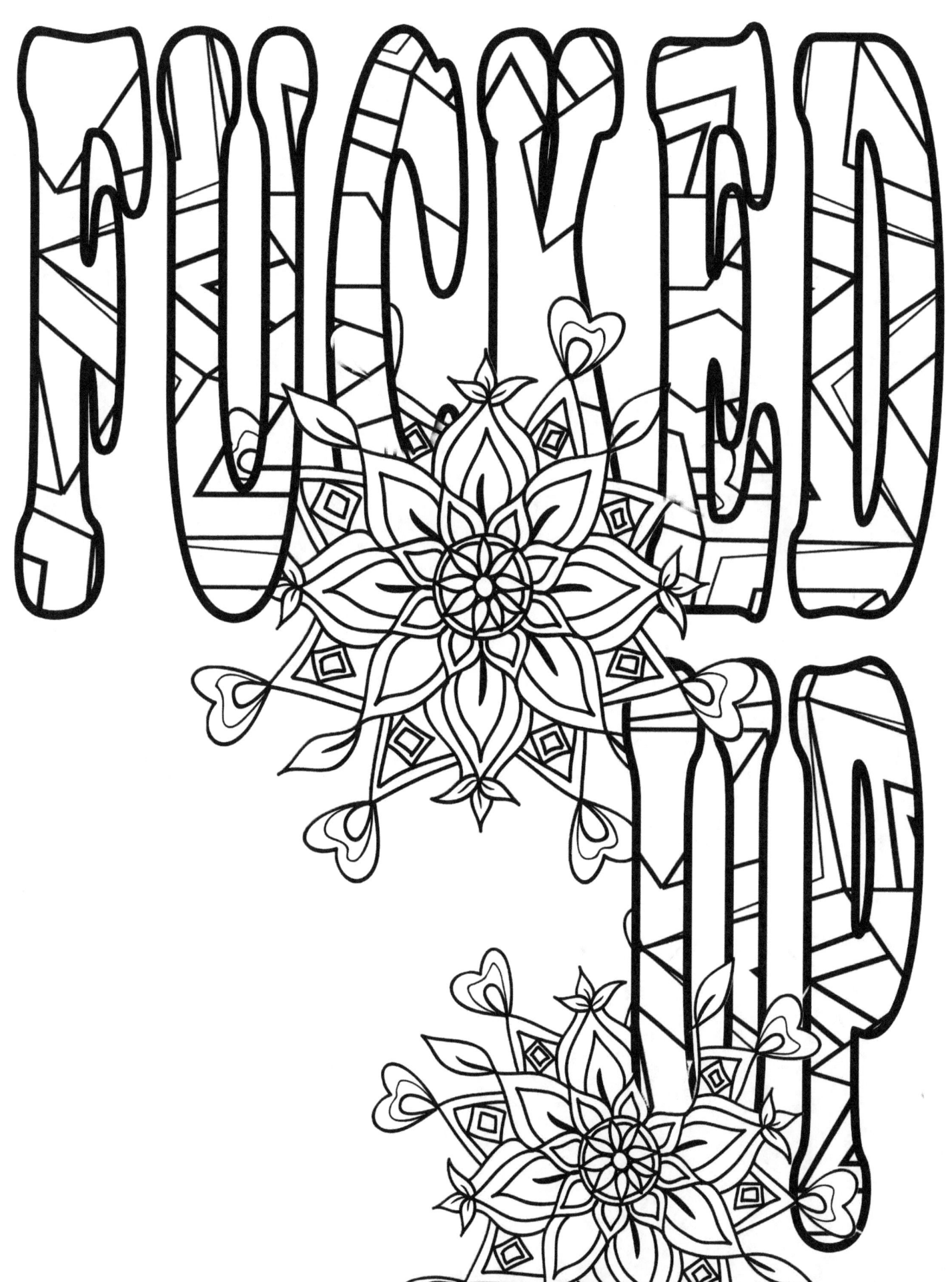

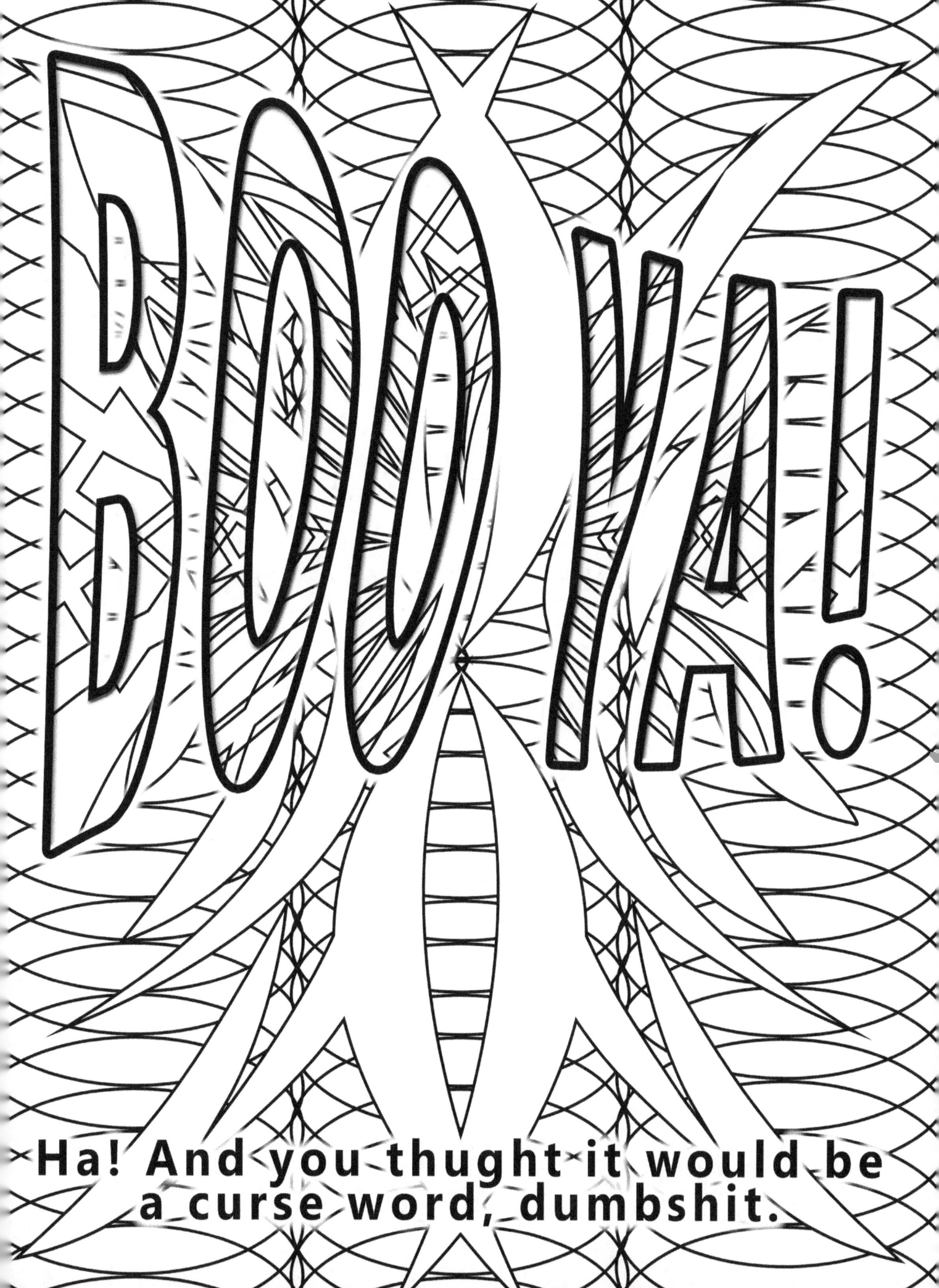

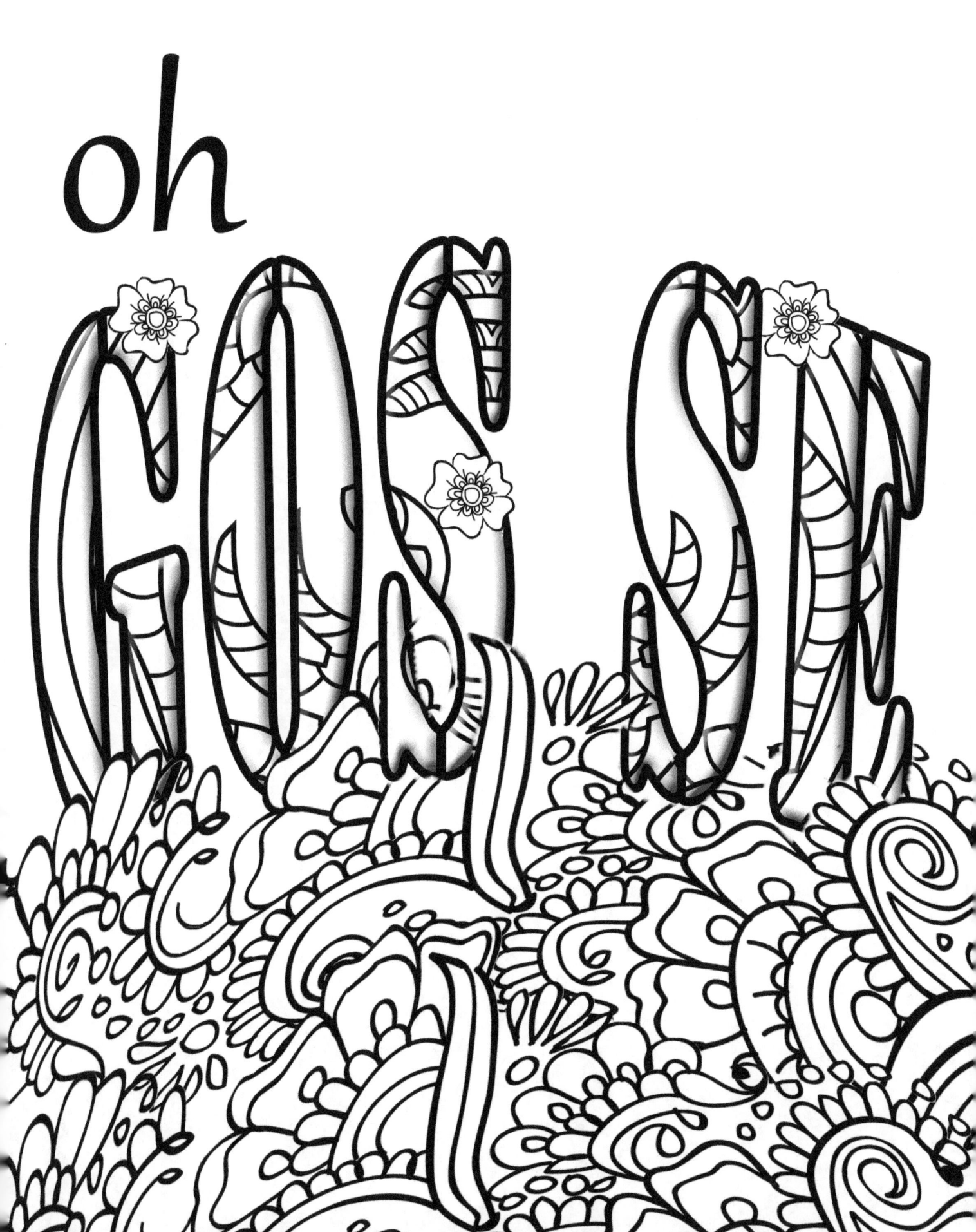

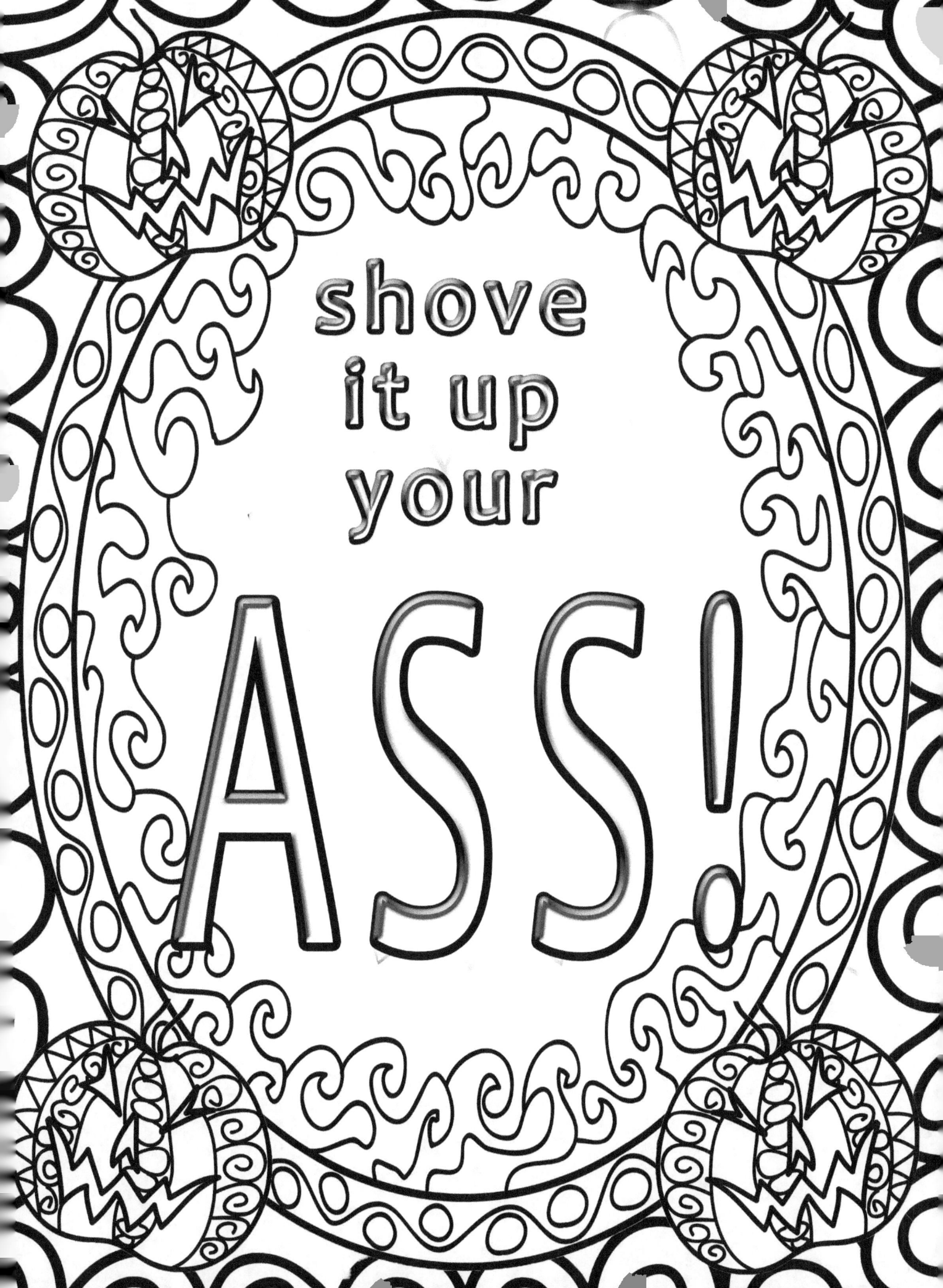

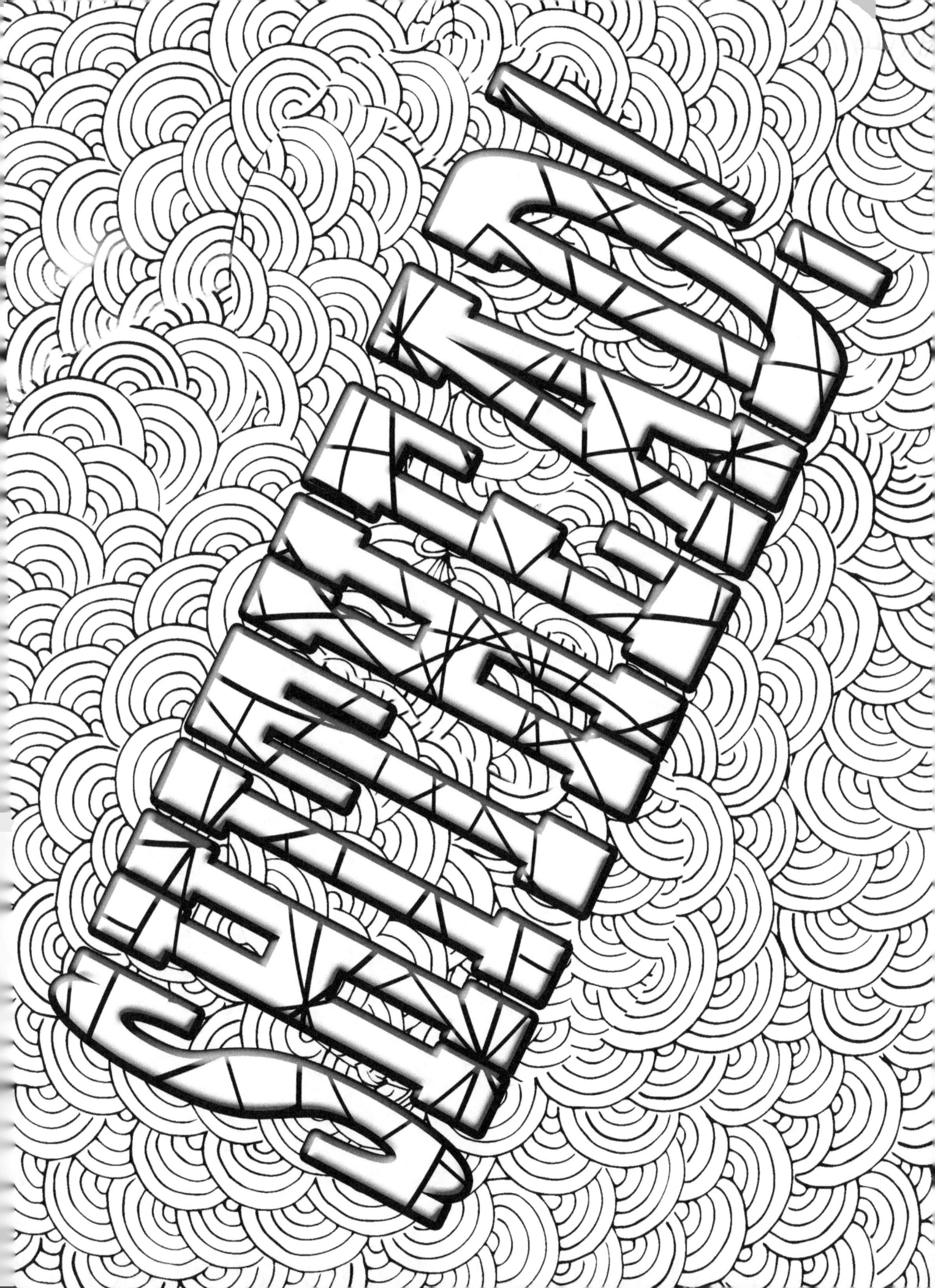

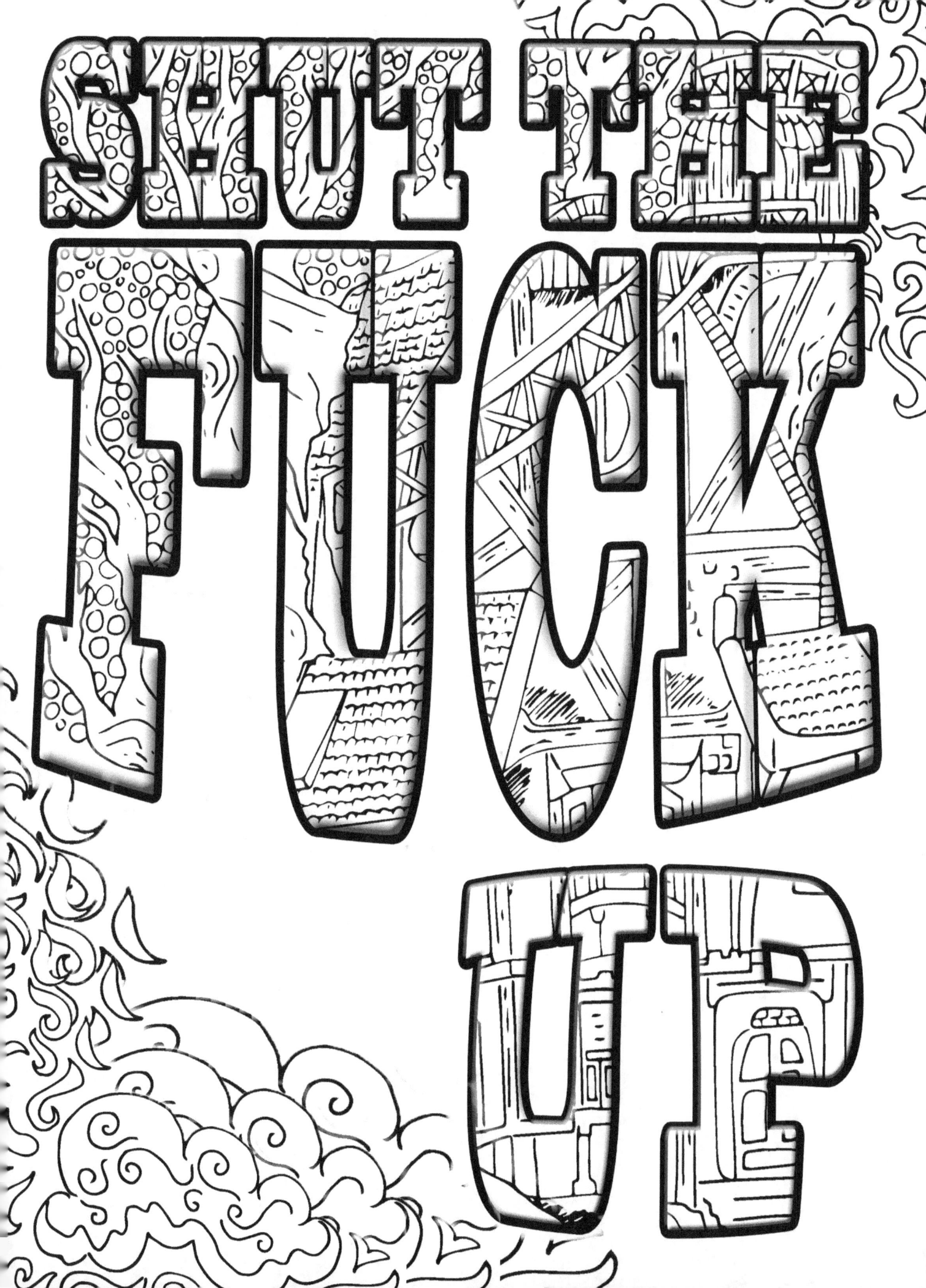

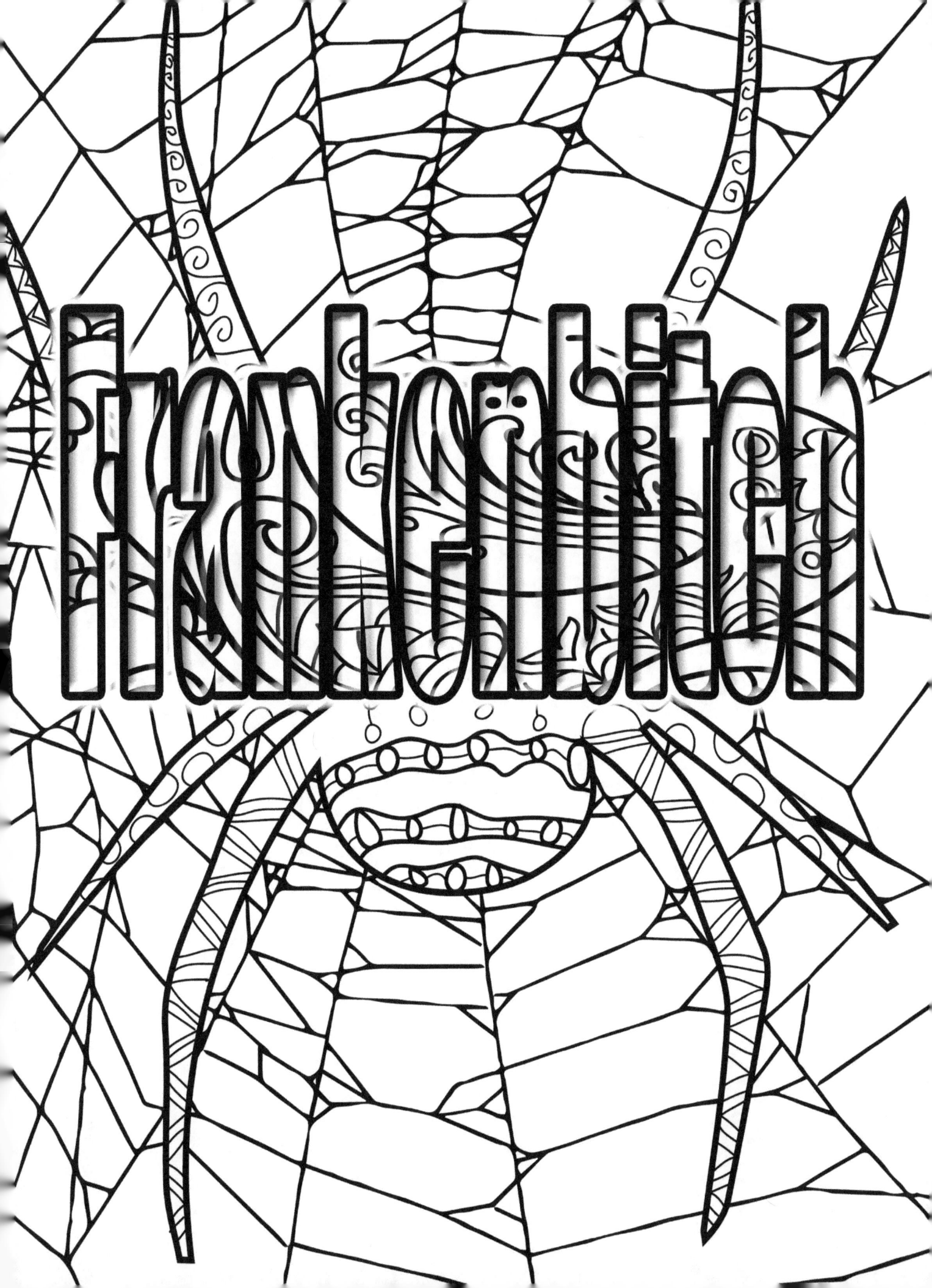

hey

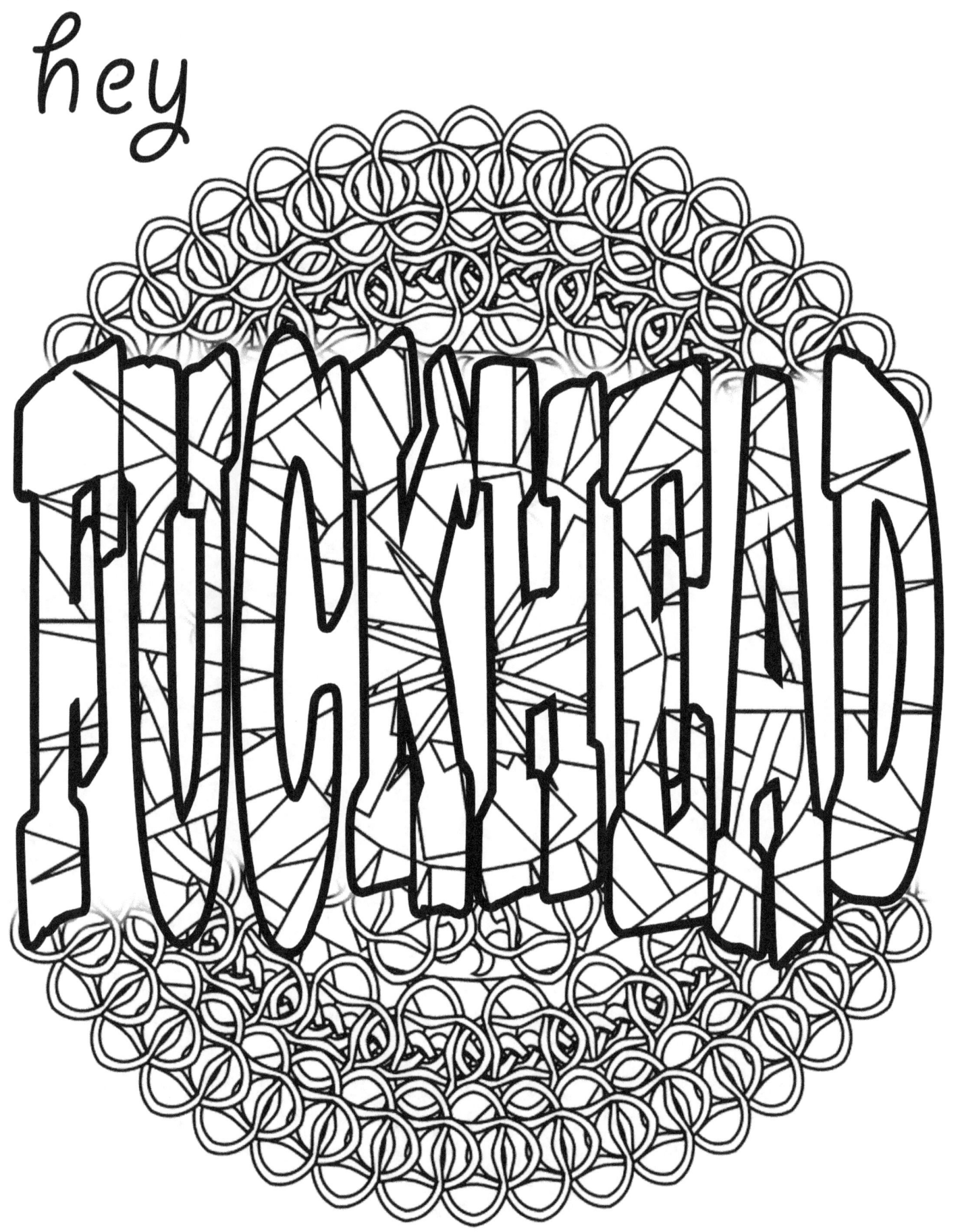

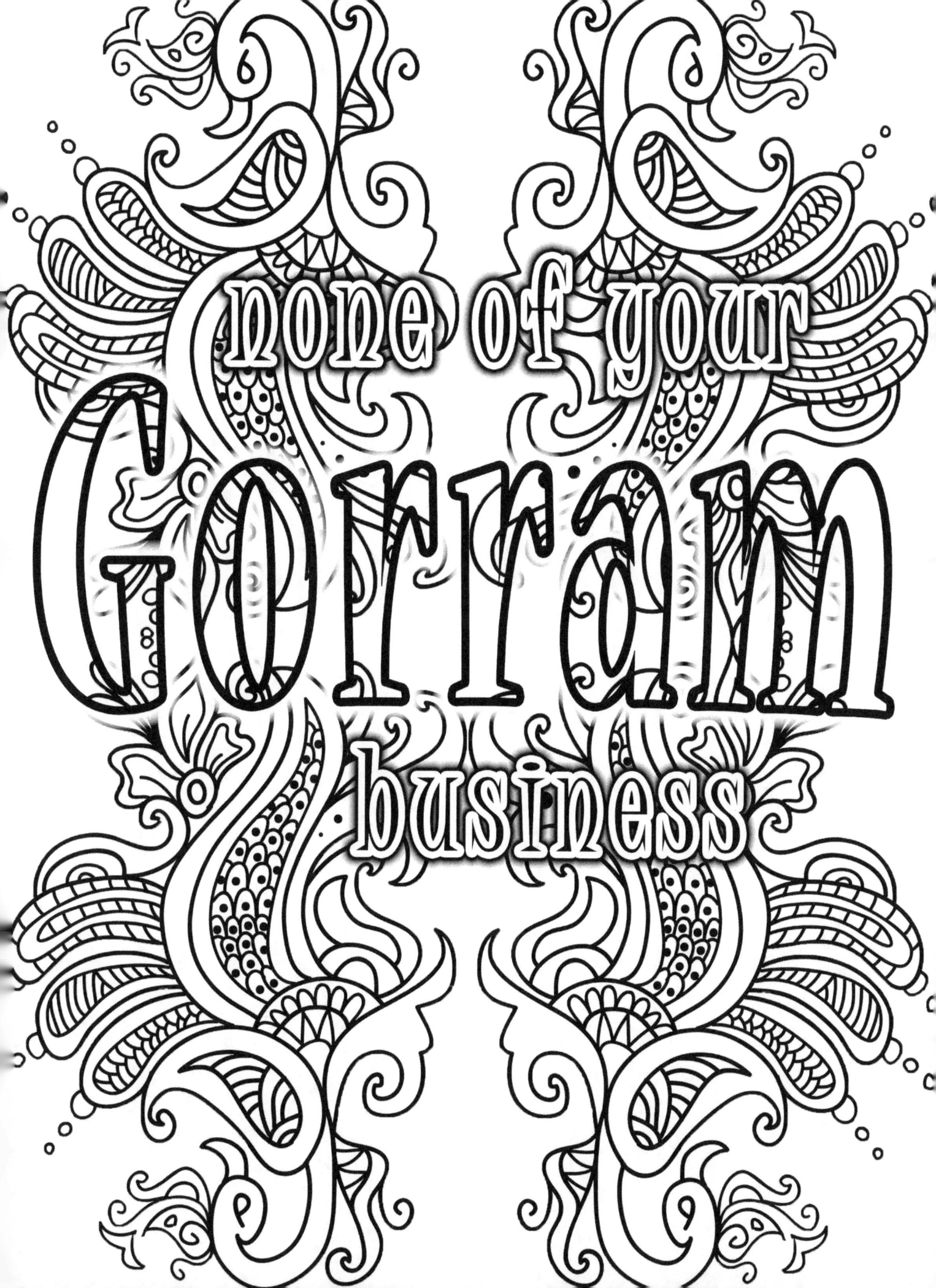

I'd empathize, but I don't give a
SHIT!

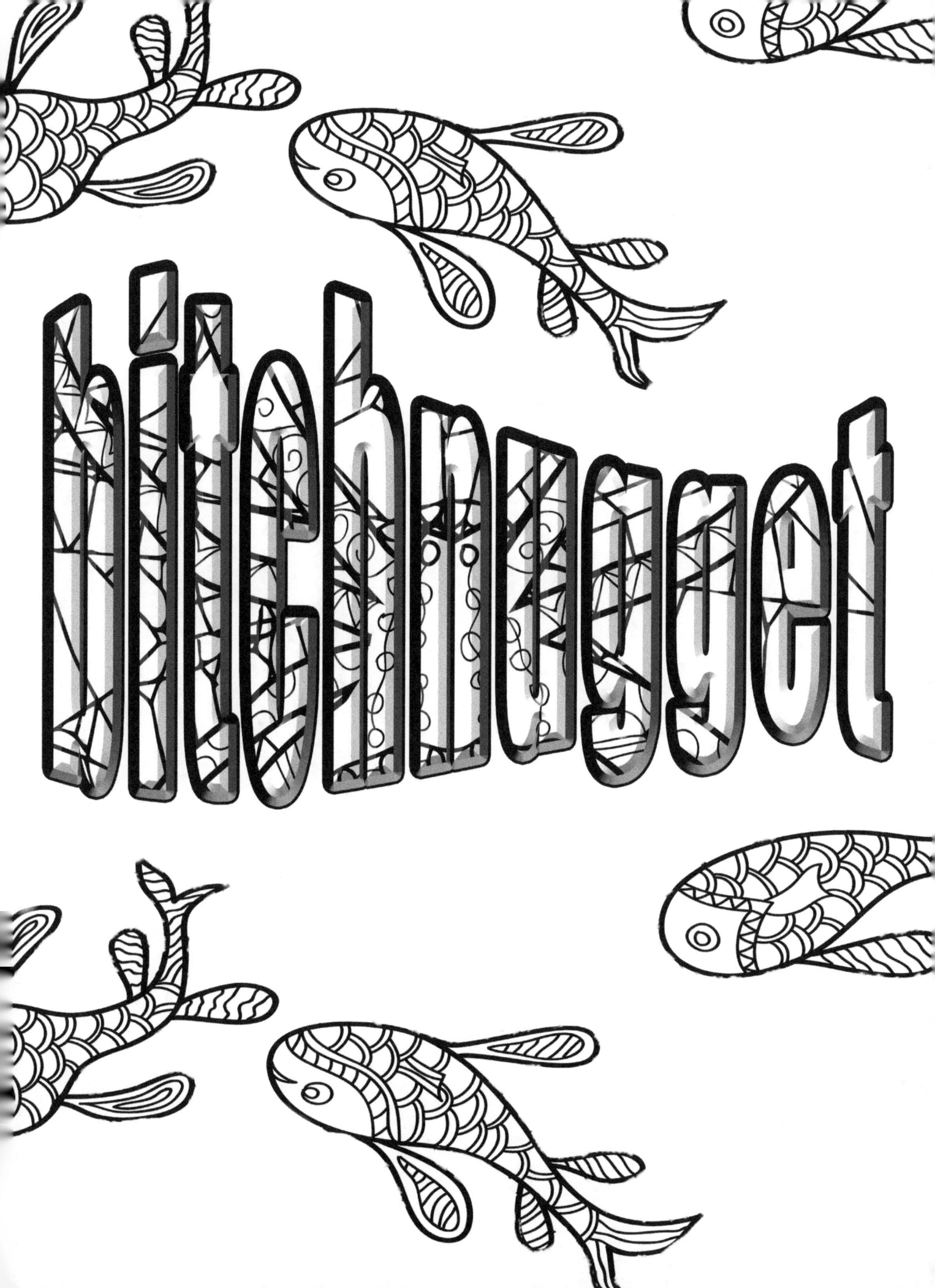

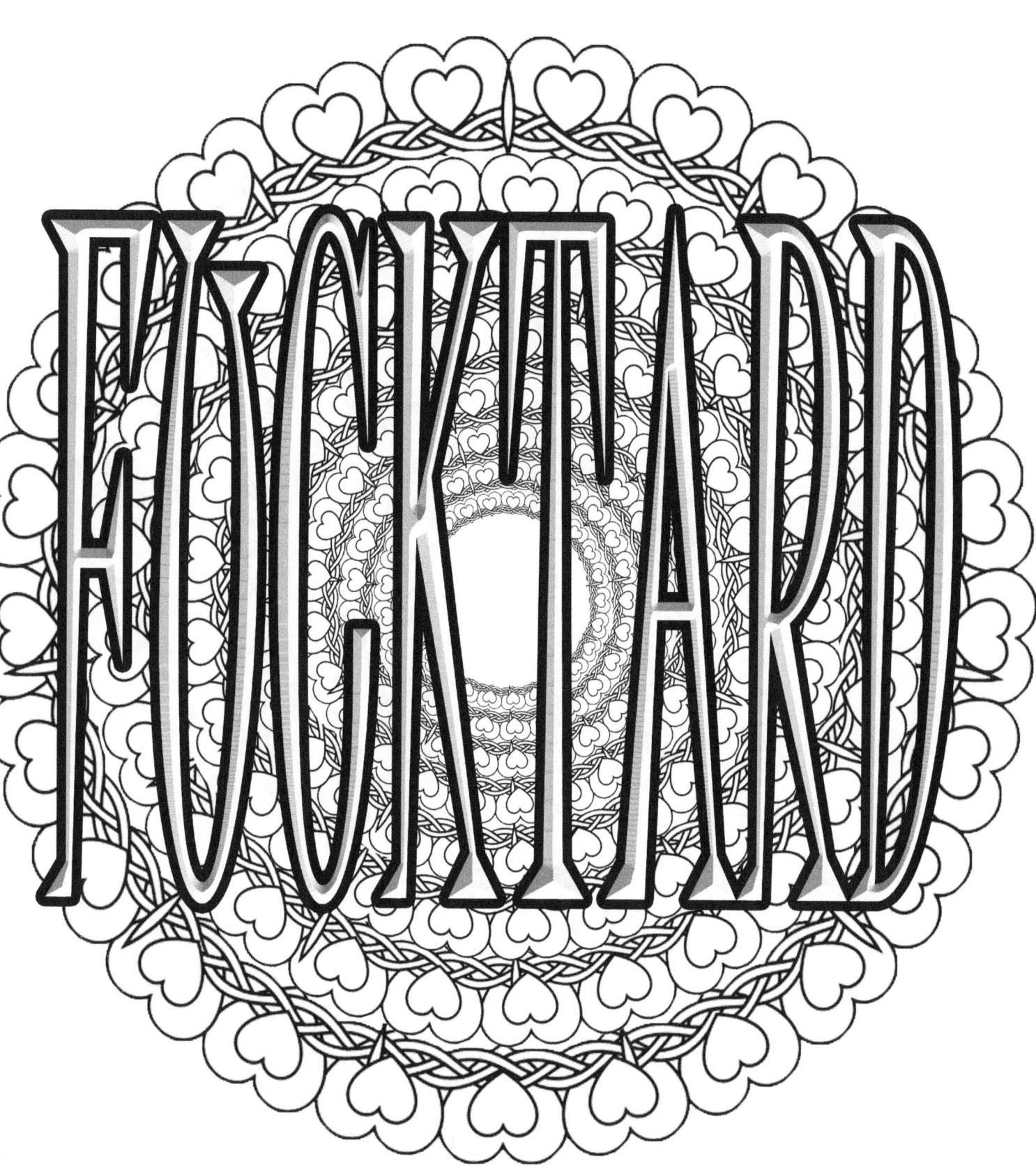

More in the Adult Coloring Book series...

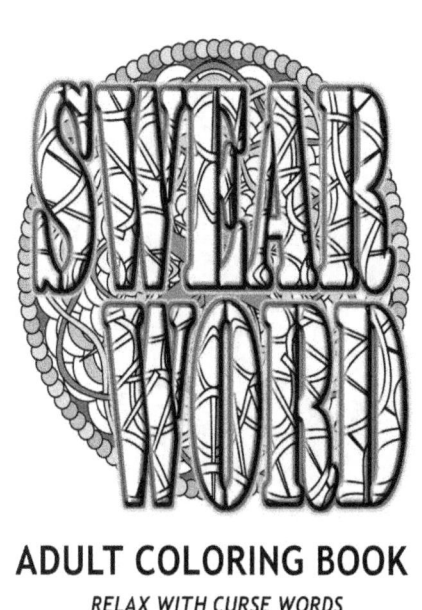

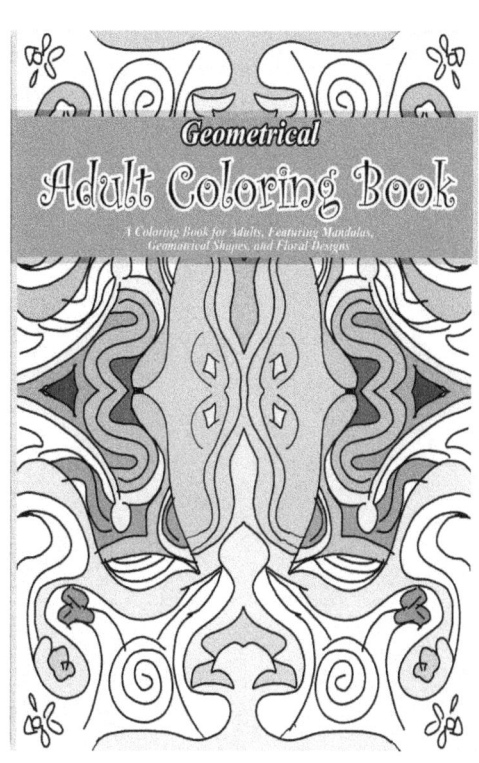

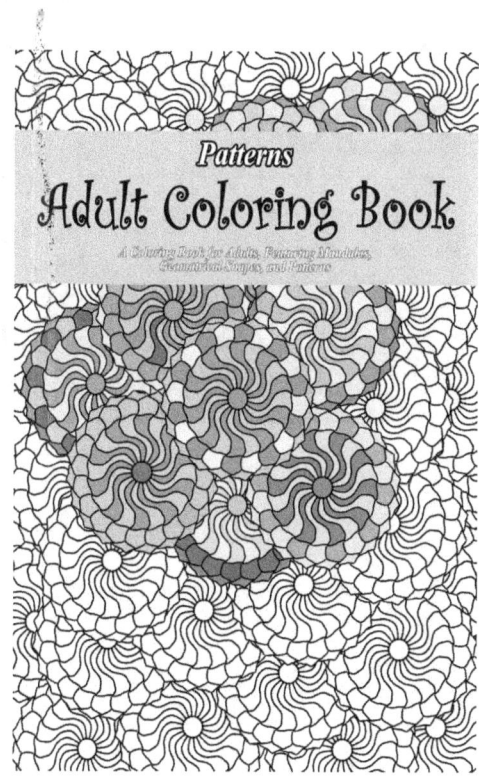

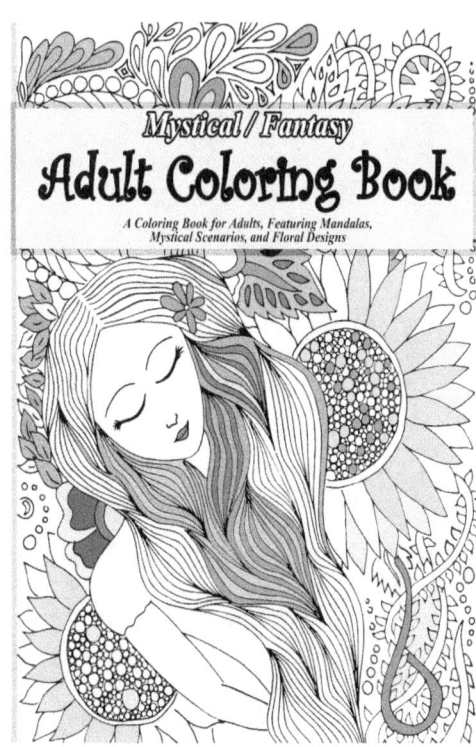

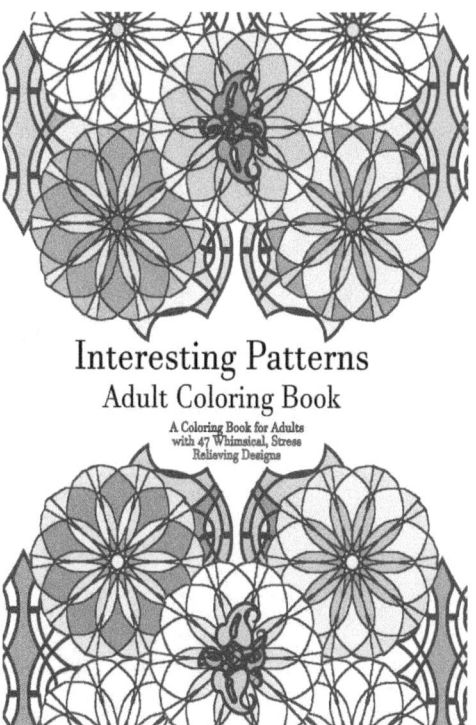

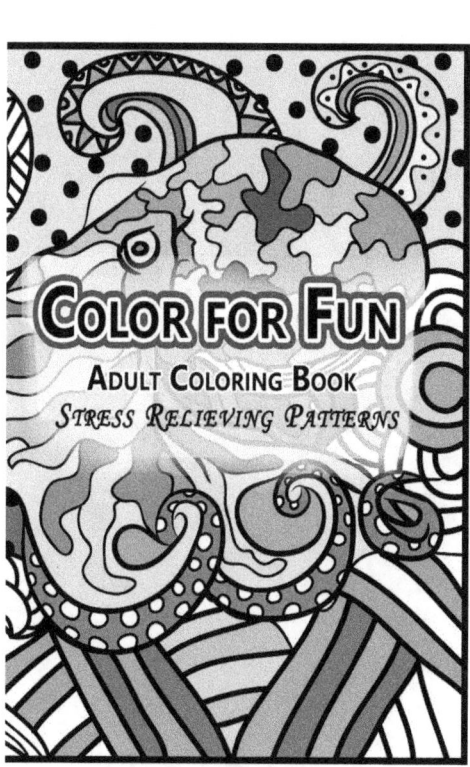

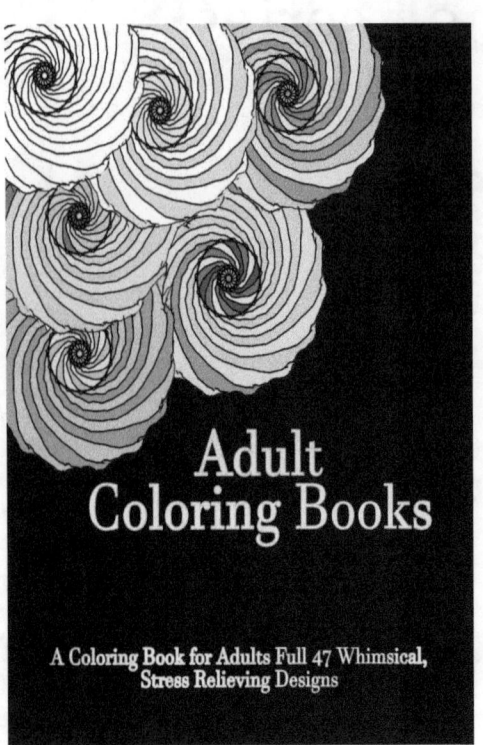

Adult
Coloring Books

A Coloring Book for Adults Full 47 Whimsical,
Stress Relieving Designs